STRESEMANN and the Rearmament of Germany

HANS W. GATZKE

STRESEMANN
and the
Rearmament
of Germany

Baltimore | THE JOHNS HOPKINS PRESS

TO James S. and Dorothea W. Smith

Preface

This study is based on the unpublished papers of Dr. Gustav Stresemann, which came into Allied possession at the end of World War II as part of the vast collection of German Foreign Ministry documents. They were opened to research in the spring of 1953, as the result of a U. S.–British agreement. The chief credit for effecting the release of these papers from the German Foreign Ministry Documents Project (sponsored by the U. S., British, and French governments) belongs to the German Documents Branch of the U. S. Department of State. Its members, being scholars themselves, have shown real understanding for the needs of scholarship and have tried to make available for research as many of the captured German materials as possible. Without their efforts, this book could not have been written. The author is indebted, furthermore, to his colleagues of the Johns Hopkins history department for sharing some of his teaching duties, so he could devote his time to research and writing. In addition, Professors Sidney Painter and David Spring gave invaluable advice, especially on matters of style and organization. Dr. Fritz Epstein of the Library of Congress, Professor Edward Fox of Cornell University, Professor Raymond Sontag of the University of California at Berkeley, and Dr. Annelise Thimme each read and criticized the manuscript, making many pertinent observations and useful suggestions. In addition, Miss Thimme kindly permitted the author to read the manuscript of her forthcoming biography of Stresemann. The careful scrutiny of the manuscript by Miss Lilly Lavarello and Mr. Kenneth Munzert, finally, resulted in the detection of many stylistic blemishes and inconsistencies. The author is grateful to all the above for making this a better book. He also wishes to thank the staffs of the National Archives in Washington and of the History Library of The Johns Hopkins University for their constant and friendly helpfulness, and the *New York Times* for supplying and giving permission to use the frontispiece of the book.

H. W. G.

Contents

STRESEMANN and the Rearmament of Germany

I | Introduction

THE TERM "REARMAMENT" in the title of this study is meant to cover a wide field—from mere evasion of the disarmament clauses of the Treaty of Versailles to actual rearmament, both within Germany and on foreign soil, notably in the Soviet Union. The fact of these violations is by now generally accepted, although their complete history still needs to be written.[1] Compared to similar activities under Hitler, these pre-1933 rearmament ventures, quantitatively speaking, were slight indeed. But this does not detract from their importance in supplying the blueprint and actual framework without which the rise of the Nazi Wehrmacht would have been significantly retarded.[2] By necessity the rearmament of the Reichswehr had to be secret, concealed from the hostile eyes of foreign observers and domestic (mostly left-wing) critics. Yet it would be wrong to conclude from this emphasis on secrecy, that the violations of the Versailles disarmament provisions were carried on exclusively by the army and behind the back or against the protest of

[1] J. H. Morgan, *Assize of Arms* (London, 1945), set out to do this, but only the first and more general of his two projected volumes has appeared, and the publication of the more important second volume has been abandoned. See also: Telford Taylor, *Sword and Swastika* (New York, 1952), ch. II; Walter Görlitz, *Der Deutsche Generalstab* (Frankfurt a. M., 1950), ch. IX; and John Wheeler-Bennett, *The Nemesis of Power* (London, 1953), chs. II and III.

[2] Görlitz, *Generalstab*, p. 359, and B. H. Liddell Hart, *The German Generals Talk* (New York, 1948), pp. 13-14, hold that pre-Hitlerian rearmament has been "overrated," a view not shared by Morgan, Taylor, and Wheeler-Bennett.

3

Germany's civilian authorities. There is sufficient evidence that
the leading members of each cabinet had at least a general
knowledge of, and in some cases even lent active support to,
the Reichswehr's clandestine operations.[3] How far this collu-
sion went can be seen in the case of Gustav Stresemann, the
Weimar Republic's outstanding political figure, Chancellor for
a hundred days in 1923, and Foreign Minister for more than
six crucial years until his death in 1929. The fact that Stresemann is considered the leading exponent of Germany's policy of
"fulfillment," "a fighter for international understanding and
world peace," and a forerunner of present efforts towards a
United Europe, adds special interest to a study of his relations
to Germany's secret rearmament.

Almost all the writings on Stresemann, partly from bias, more
often from lack of evidence, entirely ignore this side of his
activities;[4] or if they do mention it, try to explain it away.[5] The
three published volumes of the Foreign Minister's papers do not
yield much evidence either, since they were carefully edited
by his trusted friend and secretary, Henry Bernhard.[6] It was
only with the opening to research in early 1953 of Stresemann's
collected papers, that more material on this important subject
became available.[7] A still more significant source, the documents

[3] See Hans Rothfels' introduction to Helm Speidel, "Reichswehr und
Rote Armee," *Vierteljahrshefte für Zeitgeschichte*, I, No. 1 (January 1953),
p. 16.

[4] The many biographies of Stresemann, while differing in quality, are alike
in their exclusive emphasis on the peaceful aspects of his policy and personality. Written by friends or admirers, their value to the historian is slight.
The most informative is Walter Görlitz, *Gustav Stresemann* (Heidelberg,
1947). For the rest consult the bibliographical essay below, pp. 117 ff. The
book worthy of the subject has yet to be written.

[5] Felix E. Hirsch, "Stresemann in Historical Perspective," *Review of
Politics*, XV, No. 3 (July 1953), pp. 375 ff.

[6] Gustav Stresemann, *Vermächtnis. Der Nachlass in drei Bänden*, ed. by
Henry Bernhard (Berlin, 1932-33).

[7] Germany, Auswärtiges Amt, Politisches Archiv, "Nachlass des Reichs-

of the German Foreign Office for the Weimar period, is not as
yet open to private scholars.[8] The available evidence, however,
is sufficient to illuminate a subject which up to now has been
the source of much controversy between Stresemann's friends
and critics.[9]

Stresemann emerged from the war shaken by defeat and the
fall of the monarchy which came to him as a complete surprise.
He had not seen military service, for physical reasons; but as
the leading member of the National Liberal Party he had firmly
supported Germany's military and naval leaders on such vital
issues as war aims and unrestricted submarine warfare.[10] During
the early postwar years, he remained an ardent nationalist, too
loyal to disavow overnight the things he had believed in for
so long. "I know," he wrote to Oberst Bauer, Ludendorff's
right-hand man, "that people are looking for a scapegoat and
hope to find it in Ludendorff. But I shall not be a party to
that."[11] He attacked the removal of Hindenburg's pictures from
the walls of government offices (where they might offend foreign
observers) as "spineless cringing"; and in general he castigated

ministers Dr. Gustav Stresemann," microfilm, National Archives, Washington,
D. C. (cited hereafter as Stresemann, "Nachlass"). For an analysis of these
papers, see Hans W. Gatzke, "The Stresemann Papers," *Journal of Modern
History*, XXVI, No. 1 (March 1954), pp. 49-59. Henry L. Bretton, *Stresemann and the Revision of Versailles* (Stanford, 1953), had access to the
"Nachlass" and devotes a brief chapter to "Disarmament and Revision,"
pp. 138-149.

[8] Professor Raymond J. Sontag, who has seen these documents, has answered
in the affirmative this writer's question about Stresemann's awareness of
Germany's illegal rearmament: see *American Historical Review*, LV, No. 3
(April 1950), p. 738.

[9] For a strongly critical view of Stresemann, see K. Fritz Bieligk, *Stresemann.
The German Liberals' Foreign Policy* (London, 1944).

[10] Hans W. Gatzke, *Germany's Drive to the West—A Study of Germany's
Western War Aims during the First World War* (Baltimore, 1950), *passim*;
Görlitz, *Stresemann*, pp. 59 ff.

[11] Stresemann, "Nachlass," container 3068, serial 6889, frame 133554
(cited hereafter as 3068/6889/133554); *ibid.*, 3096/7018/144526.

the "Byzantine attitude" shown by many of his contemporaries towards the Republic.[12]   Certainly in his heart Stresemann guarded a deep veneration, heavily colored with romanticism, for Germany's impressive military past. Even in later years the mere spectacle of changing guards could bring tears to his eyes.[13]   In a letter to the former German Crown Prince as late as 1922, he suggested the following production for staging at Berlin's "Metropol" theater: It should first present the new Germany after November 9, 1918; and then, in form of a "vision" give a picture of the past, "the old Kaiser [William I] at his historic window, and marching past him in *Parademarsch* the guards, to the tune of their old marches." The audience, he added, would rise and cheer.[14] [Stresemann, as a recent biographer points out, never really learned to see the Germany before 1918 in its true colors but looked back upon it with the nostalgia common to so many of his generation.] To that extent he never grew up but maintained "a certain youthfulness which, according to contemporaries, exuded its special charm." [15]

Stresemann's monarchist sentiments and his friendly relations with the Crown Prince, whom he helped return from exile, are too well known to need retelling.[16]   He also kept up his wartime contacts with Ludendorff, and only broke them after 1923, when the General became increasingly involved in radically rightist and *völkisch* activities, thus scattering, as Stresemann put it, "the laurels he had garnered during the war." [17]   Through-

---

[12] *Ibid.*, 3096/7018/144528.

[13] Edgar Stern-Rubarth, *Drei Männer suchen Europa—Briand, Chamberlain, Stresemann* (Munich, 1947), p. 59.

[14] Stresemann, "Nachlass," 3110/7012/143697.

[15] Annelise Thimme, "Gustav Stresemann, Im Kampf um den Weimarer Staat," ch. I. Miss Thimme kindly permitted the author to read this manuscript of her forthcoming book.

[16] Stresemann, *Vermächtnis*, I, 215-224.

[17] Stresemann, "Nachlass," 3095/7004/142701; *ibid.*, 3110/7009/143403; *ibid.*, 3110/7011/143580 ff.

out the 1920's, Stresemann carried on an intermittent correspondence with some of the leading participants in the Kapp
Putsch of 1920, notably Pabst and Lüttwitz. These men con-
tinually reminded him of the promise he and several other party
leaders had made at that time to work towards an eventual
amnesty for the Kapp conspirators.[18] Lüttwitz, at one point,
wrote that Stresemann had not shown "an exactly negative
interest" in the Putsch,[19] and Pabst even claimed that he had
been "privy to" (*Mitwisser*) the affair.[20] A recent study shows
that the role of Stresemann and his party in helping to wind up
the Kapp Putsch with the least possible harm to the conspirators
was dictated by the fear of a possible communist uprising,
touched off by the General Strike, which in turn might have
led to a catastrophe rather than a mere defeat for the right and
to far-reaching social, political, and military changes.[21]

Given Stresemann's associations and opinions, it is not surprising that he was sympathetic towards the army's early efforts
at evading or violating the military restrictions of the Treaty of
Versailles. The surrender to the French of some special weapons
he branded as "treason" and he swore to see to it that the guilty
official was called to account.[22] Attempts to exceed the limit of
100,000 men imposed by the Treaty met with his approval.
He favored the formation of local "citizen guards" (*Einwohnerwehren*) and their consolidation into the "Orgesch" by the

---

[18] *Ibid.*, 3090/6929/139080; *ibid.*, 3110/7011/143514; *ibid.*, 3110/7013/
143907 f.; *ibid.*, 3106/7166/155063 ff.; *ibid.*, 3117/7169/155730 ff.; *ibid.*,
3143/7313/158817. These are just a few of the letters, and many more could
be cited.

[19] Stresemann, "Nachlass," 3110/7011/143514.

[20] *Ibid.*, 3117/7169/155730 ff. Pabst will reappear at a later stage in
Stresemann's career: see below, pp. 51 ff.

[21] Erich Heinz Schlottner, *Stresemann, der Kapp Putsch und die Ereignisse
in Mitteldeutschland und in Bayern im Herbst 1923* (Frankfurt a. M., 1948),
ch. I.

[22] Stresemann, "Nachlass," 3109/6998/141612.

Bavarian Forstrat Escherisch.[23] (Stresemann corresponded and maintained close relations with Escherisch until shortly before the latter's death.[24]) In correspondence with the inspector of Prussia's "Security Police" (Sipo), von Priesdorff, the latter initiated Stresemann into his plans for making the police a haven for former officers, thus keeping it free from radical contamination.[25] In 1921, when the army fell behind in its payments to the Upper Silesian "Free Corps," the latter turned to Stresemann; and in return for his help on this and other occasions he was awarded their own special decoration by the Oberschlesienkämpfer. This he later returned, since he had not participated in any of the actual fighting and felt that he did not deserve such an honor.[26] Any dissolution or disarmament of these illegal formations was opposed by Stresemann and his German People's Party, partly because Germany's eastern frontiers would thus be left exposed to a possible Polish invasion, but more importantly because such measures might "undermine the predominance of the bourgeoisie" and lead to "domination by the communist masses." It was this same fear, as we have said, that had determined Stresemann's attitude during the Kapp Putsch. For Stresemann and his party followers the army presented the only really effective protection for the existing economic and social order against possible socialization or bolshevization. And his role as arbiter during the Kapp Putsch should be seen as an effort to prevent a weakening of that protective force, split on this occasion between the forces of Lüttwitz and the Reichswehr. There was the danger, Stresemann explained,

[23] *Ibid.*, 3089/6925/138316. On the "Orgesch" (Organisation Escherisch), see Robert G. L. Waite, *Vanguard of Nazism, The Free Corps Movement in Post-War Germany 1918-1923* (Cambridge, Mass., 1952), pp. 198-199.

[24] Stresemann, "Nachlass," 3114/7135/149029; *ibid.*, 3144/7325/161126; *ibid.*, 3177/7388/170150.

[25] *Ibid.*, 3089/6926/138546, 138556.

[26] *Ibid.*, 3094/7001/142168; *ibid.*, 3109/6997/141342; *ibid.*, 3109/6998/141720 ff.

"if everyone turned against this kind of militarism, that the Social Democrats might get a chance to abolish the Reichswehr, arm the workers, and thus put the republican people's army into the saddle." [27] To avert this danger, Stresemann, in 1921, wished for a rightist cabinet, which would place the important Ministry of the Interior into reliable middle-class hands.[28]

As time went on, the undercover activities of the Reichswehr changed from passive obstruction of disarmament to more active measures of rearmament. At this stage the aid of certain large industrialists (notably Krupp) and of Soviet Russia emerged as decisive factors.[29] Russo-German military contacts can be traced with certainty back to early 1921; [30] and the first agreement

[27] Schlottner, *Stresemann*, pp. 34-38.

[28] Stresemann, "Nachlass," 3091/6933/139793-94; *ibid.*, 3093/6994/140865 ff. Actually the disagreement over military matters between the right and left was not as serious as might appear from these statements. Prussia's socialist Minister of the Interior, Severing, while "shuddering" at the hidden stores of arms and the instances of collaboration between the army and illegal rightist formations, was chiefly worried lest these arms and men might be used in an uprising against the government. In an agreement which Minister of Defense Gessler and Severing signed on June 30, 1923, the latter promised his full co-operation in saving weapons and other equipment for Reichswehr use. He also agreed to the training of volunteers in excess of the legal maximum as long as they were recruited from among loyal supporters of the Republic. The army subsequently violated this agreement repeatedly. But the glowing tribute which Gessler paid Severing upon the latter's retirement in 1926 showed that such violations did not seriously disturb their relationship: Carl Severing, *Mein Lebensweg* (2 vols., Cologne, 1950), II, 114-139; see also E. J. Gumbel, "*Verräter verfallen der Feme*," *Opfer, Mörder, Richter 1919-1929* (Berlin, 1929), pp. 254-255.

[29] Germany's efforts to evade the Versailles terms assumed many forms. Görlitz, *Generalstab*, pp. 359-360, distinguishes the following: relations between Reichswehr and Russia; illegal formations on the eastern borders; training of excess men and preparations for their mobilization; illegal economic preparations of a military nature; development of prohibited weapons (heavy artillery, tanks) and completely new weapons; creation of a secret air force; and illegal activities in the naval field (U-boats, PT boats, naval air force).

[30] Edward Hallet Carr, *German-Soviet Relations between the Two World Wars 1919-1939* (Baltimore, 1951), pp. 56-57. The original idea of Russo-

between the firm of Krupp and the Defense Ministry to circumvent the military restrictions of Versailles was concluded in January of 1922.[31] The Ruhr crisis in 1923 brought a general acceleration of undercover military development, a good deal of it with the support of civilian authorities. Yet it is doubtful that any civilian (including the Minister of Defense) was ever fully initiated into the army's darkest secrets. "We were as secretive towards our own government," General Blomberg once wrote, "as we were against supervision by our enemies." There is no evidence that Stresemann, prior to his appointment as Chancellor on August 13, 1923, shared any of these deeper secrets, much as he was in sympathy with the army's persistent stand against the Treaty of Versailles.

German military collaboration, however, can be traced back as far as the last days of the war. In August 1918, a series of supplementary economic agreements to the Treaty of Brest Litovsk were discussed between a German group (Nadolny, von Prittwitz, Count Kessler, Litwin, and Stresemann) and Soviet representatives (Joffe and Krassin). It was hoped that such agreements would gradually lead to a military alliance with Russia, which was stated as their chief aim: Stresemann, "Nachlass," 3077/6912/136131 ff., 136169 ff., 136249 ff.; ibid., 3077/6911/135887, 135896 ff., 135973 ff., 136002 ff.

[31] Germany, U. S. Zone of Occupation, Military Tribunals, Trials of War Criminals before the Nürnberg Military Tribunals (Washington, D. C., Government Printing Office, 1950), IX, 274.

II | From Ruhr to Locarno

ONE OF THE FIRST acts of Stresemann, after he became Chancellor, was to go to Döberitz to pay a visit to the officers of the Reichswehr, since the army, in his opinion, was "the only positive factor" in Germany at that time. The head of the Reichswehr, the man who had created and who jealously guarded this new force through its initial years, tight-lipped, frozen-faced General Hans von Seeckt, was waiting to greet the new Chancellor. The first impression Stresemann made was not too bad; at least he gave a "skillful" reply to Seeckt's welcoming speech.[1] "He is no doubt a very agile and also good politician," the general had commented after an earlier meeting, but "I have no close relations with him and shall not seek any."[2]

If this statement indicates an initial reserve toward Stresemann on Seeckt's part, this soon turned into outright opposition. There are several reasons for this.[3] In many respects it was merely the current manifestation of the traditional tension between top civilian and military authorities, for which German history from Bismarck to Bethmann Hollweg showed many precedents. As Seeckt's friend and biographer Rabenau puts it: "The

[1] Friedrich von Rabenau, *Seeckt: Aus seinem Leben 1918-1936* (Leipzig, 1940), pp. 335-336.
[2] *Ibid.*, p. 350.
[3] Seeckt's friend General Rabenau, and Stresemann's friend Konsul Bernhard each have given us their quite different view of the Seeckt-Stresemann relationship: Rabenau, *Seeckt*, pp. 355, 406, and *passim*; Henry Bernhard, "Seeckt und Stresemann," *Deutsche Rundschau*, LXXIX, No. 5 (May 1953), pp. 465-474.

Chancellors after Cuno were no longer taken quite seriously by Seeckt. They changed too often. . . ."[4] More specifically, Stresemann's gradualist approach of revising the Treaty of Versailles by "undermining" (aushöhlen) it, not only was foreign but probably incomprehensible to Seeckt's military mind.[5] "We must regain our power," the latter once said, "and as soon as we do, we naturally will take back everything we lost."[6] Stresemann, for his part, was opposed to any kind of "bragging and sabre-rattling without a sabre."[7] Furthermore, while his policy showed a decidedly western orientation, Seeckt "was inspired by a deeply rooted aversion to France," and instead looked to collaboration with Russia as a way out of Germany's predicaments.[8] But equally, if not more important than these specific differences was the general contrast in background between the soldier and "Junker of ancient and noble lineage," Seeckt, and the civilian and offspring of a small retailer of bottled beer, Stresemann. Their very appearance merely emphasized that difference: Stresemann—stout, jovial, and talkative; Seeckt—slim, severe, and silent. Stresemann, admirer of things Prussian and military that he was, once characterized his feeling towards Seeckt as one of "unhappy love."[9] Seeckt, on his part, repaid with all the arrogance and snobbery that his class could muster against commoners. There is a ring of spite in the rare references Seeckt made in letters to his wife about the Stresemanns: "Tea at

[4] Rabenau, Seeckt, p. 355.

[5] Stresemann, "Nachlass," 3167/7338/163684.

[6] Ibid., 3113/7129/147890.

[7] Ibid., 3099/7118/145903.

[8] George W. F. Hallgarten, "General Hans von Seeckt and Russia, 1920-1922," Journal of Modern History, XXI, No. 1 (March 1949), p. 28. Hans Herzfeld, Das Problem des Deutschen Heeres 1919-1945 (Laupheim, 1952), pp. 8-10.

[9] Rabenau, Seeckt, p. 335. There is little evidence in the Stresemann "Nachlass" for Bernhard's statement ("Seeckt und Stresemann," p. 466) that these papers contain "many a harsh judgment" of Stresemann on Seeckt.

Madame's . . . in velvet and lace—she, not he. They say he spoke brilliantly today, but his parliamentary death is prophesied for tomorrow." [10]

This discord between two such key figures naturally had far-reaching political consequences. Stresemann, at the start, tried to convert Seeckt to his own views on foreign policy; but such efforts were branded by Seeckt as mere attempts to find an "accomplice." [11] Seeckt welcomed (and may have conspired in) Stresemann's "resignation" as Chancellor on November 23, 1923, though he failed in his efforts to have him retired from the foreign ministership as well. [12] The general did support Stresemann's first major venture in foreign policy, the Dawes Plan, but he did so for reasons of his own and not because he favored a "policy of fulfillment." [13] How much Stresemann on his side worked against Seeckt is not clear, though there can be little doubt that the general's opposition was a source of constant concern to him. A good deal of valuable time and effort was spent in asserting the Foreign Ministry's position against Reichswehr interference, much of which interference was due to Seeckt's dislike and distrust of Stresemann. How far this suspicion and hostility were carried can be seen from the fact that as late as 1926, the Reichswehr Ministry tapped Stresemann's telephone lines, chiefly to check on his policy towards

[10] Rabenau, *Seeckt*, p. 385. The *Damenkrieg* between Mrs. Seeckt (affectionately nicknamed " cat " by her husband) and Mrs. Stresemann only aggravated the strain between the two men.

[11] Rabenau, *Seeckt*, p. 335.

[12] Reginald H. Phelps, " Aus den Seeckt-Dokumenten II," *Deutsche Rundschau*, LXXVIII, No. 10 (October 1952), p. 1013. For a different view see Bernhard, " Seeckt und Stresemann," pp. 468-469.

[13] Phelps, " Aus den Seeckt-Dokumenten II," pp. 1014-1015; Rabenau, *Seeckt*, pp. 404-405. One of the incidental results of the Dawes Plan was to bring about a welcome reduction of occupation forces in the Rhineland, due to the fact that their upkeep henceforth had to be borne by the Allies themselves.

France.[14] The army also received daily, directly from the Reichs-post Ministry, copies of all important Foreign Ministry communications. Coded messages sent by foreign diplomats to their home governments were intercepted directly by military intelligence, which decoded them, but refused to communicate any information contained in these messages to Stresemann's department, even though the latter did not have a similar interception and decoding service.[15]

But as we turn to a closer examination of Stresemann's policy, it is ironic to discover that Seeckt's suspicion of him as an "appeaser" (Flaumacher) was really most unjust. Much as they might differ in outlook and approach, both, as Wheeler-Bennett rightly points out, "believed in and laboured for . . . the future greatness and might of Germany." Already during his hundred days as Chancellor, Stresemann had shown the same concern for the Reichswehr's future that had guided his attitude during the Kapp Putsch in 1920. The severity with which his government, in October of 1923, met the threat of leftist uprisings in Saxony and Thuringia was in marked contrast to the leniency shown towards simultaneous threats from the right in Bavaria. And while most of this difference, as far as Stresemann was concerned, was due to his conviction that the chief danger to Germany at this time came from the left rather than right, the fact that in Bavaria the army again was divided within itself (as it had been in the days of the Kapp Putsch) while in Saxony it was under attack from socialist and communist opposition forces, played its part in determining the Chancellor's policy. The Socialist Minister President of Saxony, Zeigner, not only had attacked the Reichswehr as a stronghold of monarchism and reaction, but he had also revealed publicly some of the Reichswehr's breaches of the disarmament clauses

[14] Stresemann, " Nachlass," 3100/7138/149451.
[15] Ibid., 3165/7414/175350, 175352; ibid., 3113/7129/147790; ibid., 3111/7138/149451.

of the Treaty of Versailles. It was this latter revelation which
particularly aroused Stresemann's indignation.[16] He was well
aware both of the Reichswehr's secret arrangements with Russia
and its rearmament efforts at home. And it was largely due to
his patient labors that the military fetters of Versailles, which
Seeckt one day hoped to burst by force, were gradually loosened
and finally slipped off altogether. Stresemann conveniently
supplied the diplomatic front, behind which "Seeckt perfected
his military foundation for the Greater Germany of the future." [17]
More specifically, Stresemann freed the Reichswehr from the
annoying supervision of the Inter-Allied Military Control Commission, which had been set up to check on Germany's fulfillment of the military provisions of Versailles, and about which
Seeckt had said: "The important thing for Germany is that
they [i.e., the Allied control officers] get out." As far back as
1921, Minister of Defense Gessler had asked the help of the
Foreign Ministry in liberating Germany from this "agency of
suppression." [18] It was Stresemann, as we shall see, who supplied
this help.

By the time Stresemann took office, in 1923, the Control
Commission already had been through an uninterrupted series
of major and minor fights with recalcitrant German military
officials, chiefly over Germany's failure to surrender her surplus
arms.[19] In early 1923, Britain's ambassador Lord D'Abernon had

[16] Schlottner, *Stresemann*, pp. 45-47, and *passim.* See also: Gustav Radbruch, *Der Innere Weg* (Stuttgart, 1951), pp. 172-174; Kurt Caro and
Walter Oehme, *Schleicher's Aufstieg* (Berlin, 1933), pp. 160 ff.

[17] Wheeler-Bennett, *The Nemesis of Power*, pp. 106-107.

[18] Rabenau, *Seeckt*, p. 451; Germany, Heeresarchiv Potsdam, "Papers of
General Hans von Seeckt," microfilm in Widener Library, Harvard University,
Cambridge, Massachusetts, Roll 21 (June 14, 1921).

[19] On the organization and early activities of the Allied Commission see
Morgan, *Assize of Arms, passim;* W. M. Jordan, *Great Britain, France, and
the German Problem 1918-1939* (London, 1943), pp. 135 ff.; General
C. N. E. Nollet, *Une expérience de désarmement, cinq ans de contrôle
militaire en Allemagne* (Paris, 1932), Parts I and II.

been able to write: "The work of disarmament in Germany has been carried out by the Commission of Control with skill and with surprising completeness. Notwithstanding a certain minimum of inevitable resistance and concealment, it should be added that in no other great country would an operation of disarmament have met with so little resistance as here." [20] But the ambassador had spoken too soon. All through 1923, while the Ruhr crisis was reaching its climax, Germany had refused to permit Allied inspection of her armed forces and had restricted the inspection of factories to Italian and British officers, who in turn refused to act without their French colleagues. [21] By the end of 1923, growing signs of Germany's continued evasions of her military restrictions prompted the Allied Commission to announce the resumption of its activities.

It was at this point that Stresemann first became officially involved in the matter. And from the very start he used the disingenuous technique which we shall see in operation for the next few years. To dispel Allied fears, he either tried to belittle their allegations of German rearmament, or to present excuses of various kinds for those instances of rearmament that could not be explained away. The Allies at this point were much alarmed by the continued existence of numerous rightist paramilitary organizations, their possible relations to the Reichswehr, and their equipment from hidden stores of arms. [22] On the day of

[20] Viscount D'Abernon, *The Diary of an Ambassador*, vol. II: *Rapallo to Dawes 1922-1924* (New York, 1930), p. 179. D'Abernon added the warning: " It is, indeed, probable, should the ' balance of power ' theory again become a dominant English conception of policy, that future critics will consider that a mistake has been made in 1922 in disarming Germany so far without disarming other Powers of Europe."

[21] Jordan, *German Problem*, p. 136.

[22] We cannot here go into the many different organizations by which Germany tried to exceed the numerical limits of her armed forces. Chronologically they may be tentatively arranged as follows: Free Corps (*Freikorps*) and Civil Guards (*Einwohnerwehren*), Working Associations (*Arbeitsgemeinschaften*), Black Reichswehr and Labor Groups (*Arbeitskommandos*),

the Hitler Putsch, November 9, 1923, the French Ambassador De Margerie asked Stresemann about the "quantity of rifles, guns, etc." which had been revealed by the events in Bavaria. Stresemann replied that it was "quite natural" (*selbstverständlich*) for many people in Germany to have rifles—after all, the government could not very well search each and every house. Nevertheless he denied the truth of the "fantastic numbers" often mentioned. As for renewed Allied military inspection, the Foreign Minister stated that Germany's military authorities were of the opinion that all military control was "done and over with." Certainly it would be unwise, he added, in view of popular resentment, to resume control operations at this time.[23]

A few days later, Stresemann's Secretary of State von Maltzan warned Italy's ambassador Bosdari, citing "the usual arguments," against renewed visits of the Control Commission. Such visits would so antagonize the Reichswehr that it might no longer obey the government when it came to "protecting the diplomatic corps in Berlin against excesses of the hungry mob."[24]

Finally, in early December, Stresemann told the Belgian ambassador De la Faille that the return of control officers (especially French ones) would lead to their mistreatment and perhaps death at the hands of enraged German workers from all parties. He also pointed out that Germany had far less ammunition than she was entitled to under the Versailles Treaty. As for the ambassador's fear "that Germany was busily producing war materials in preparation for the next war," Strese-

Temporary Volunteers (*Zeitfreiwillige*) and Border Guards (*Grenzschutz*). In the twilight of illegality, however, the line between these (and still other) groups is often difficult to determine. Seeckt himself speaks of the "fluidity" of the border between what he called "soldiers" and "Reichswehr soldiers": Hans von Seeckt, "Freikorps und Reichswehr," *Deutsche Tageszeitung*, May 16, 1928.

[23] Stresemann, *Vermächtnis*, I, 206.

[24] Stresemann, "Nachlass," 3099/7120/146289.

mann admitted that there were strong nationalist currents and ample manpower in Germany, but added that she lacked all implements for waging such a war.[25]

While he was thus trying to scare the Control Commission into staying away[26] or at least, by harping on the military weakness of Germany, to prove that its efforts were needless, Stresemann, in a letter to Germany's ambassador in Moscow, Brockdorff-Rantzau, painted a quite different picture: "The strong decline of socialism," he wrote, "together with the tremendous strengthening of all nationalist organizations, is a guarantee that within a foreseeable future we shall regain our strength and again become *bündnisfähig* to our friends and dangerous to our enemies."[27]

How much, we shall have to ask again and again in this study, did the Foreign Minister actually know at this time about the secret activities of the army? As we shall see later, Stresemann, upon becoming Chancellor, was informed by his predecessor Cuno of the Reichswehr's dealings with Russia.[28] We also know that Stresemann and several members of his cabinet were told, on September 11, 1923, by Saxony's Minister President Zeigner, about the relations between the Reichswehr and rightist paramilitary organizations. Stresemann condemned these relations and the formation of the illegal "Black Reichswehr" and promised to put an end to them. Yet Zeigner vainly waited for the fulfillment of these promises.[29] On November 1, Stresemann presided over a cabinet meeting at which Reichswehrminister Gessler told of the illegal increases of the Reichswehr ranks

[25] Stresemann, *Vermächtnis,* I, 263.

[26] *Ibid.,* p. 316.

[27] Stresemann, "Nachlass," 3099/7120/143310. This passage, as well as several others, has been omitted from the published version of the letter in Stresemann, *Vermächtnis,* I, 260.

[28] See below, pp. 77 ff.

[29] Caro and Oehme, *Schleicher's Aufstieg,* p. 164; Radbruch, *Der Innere Weg,* p. 174.

beyond the limits laid down at Versailles.[30] In early January 1924, the president of the pacifist *Deutsches Friendenskartell*, Professor Ludwig Quidde, addressed a letter to Seeckt in which he asked whether the many reports of the army's illegal activities were true. Seeckt refused to answer this question and threatened to have Quidde prosecuted for treason if he should pursue the matter any further. Despite this threat, the professor published his letter, together with the general's reply. The latter he considered an indirect admission that his charges were true. "It would be a surprising event," Wheeler-Bennett concludes, "if the very efficient Press Department of the German Foreign Office had not drawn the Foreign Minister's attention to so important an item of news." We now know from Stresemann's unpublished papers that such efficiency was unnecessary, since Quidde himself had sent Stresemann copies of the whole correspondence. There apparently was no reply from the Foreign Minister, who had little love for pacifists.[31] Nor is there any reply to a letter by another noted pacifist, Professor Schücking of Marburg. In March 1924 he wrote Stresemann about the activities of the "Black Reichswehr" in his district. He was deeply worried because of the danger such activities presented to the foreign policy of Stresemann, and he supported his story with evidence supplied by his students who had joined the illegal army formations in large numbers.[32]

All of Stresemann's efforts in late 1923 to prevent the resumption of Allied military control proved in vain. In early November, the Allied Conference of Ambassadors in Paris notified the German government that visits of inspection would begin without delay, and on December 30 the first of such visits was

[30] Stresemann, "Nachlass," 3099/7120/146160.

[31] Wheeler-Bennett, *The Nemesis of Power*, p. 147; Stresemann, "Nachlass," 3106/7166/155073 ff.

[32] Stresemann, "Nachlass," 3106/7167/155388.

officially announced for January 1924.[33] On January 9, Stresemann reluctantly agreed to these visits, but repeated that legally
the Control Commission's tasks had been accomplished. The
points, five to be specific, which in Allied opinion still needed
settling [34] should in his opinion not require any further inspection of military agencies; and once these points had been taken
care of, Stresemann concluded, German disarmament would be
complete. According to Article 213 of the Peace Treaty, Germany should then merely be subject to supervision by the League
Council.[35] "Control visits to check again and again on our
military strength," he stated in a personal memorandum, "go
beyond these five points and constitute a supervision of our state
of preparedness after completion of disarmament, a supervision
which . . . is exclusively the business of the League of Nations."
Though this did not mean, he added, that the League should
continue the constant supervision carried on by the Control
Commission; it should merely act on specific occasions and for
reasons clearly formulated by the League Council.[36] As we
shall see later, Stresemann considered the transfer of control

[33] C. A. Macartney et al., Survey of International Affairs 1925 (II)
(London, 1928), p. 173.

[34] As far back as September 29, 1922, the Allies had stated five categories
of control operations still to be completed: (a) the reorganization of the
police; (b) the adaptation of munitions factories to civilian production; (c)
the surrender of excess war material; (d) the delivery of statistics of the
war material in German hands at the conclusion of the Armistice; (e) the
adoption of necessary governmental measures prohibiting the import and
export of war material and adjusting the recruiting system and organization
of the Reichswehr to the terms of the Versailles Treaty: Arnold J. Toynbee,
Survey of International Affairs 1920-1923 (London, 1925), p. 112.

[35] Schulthess' Europäischer Geschichtskalender, ed. by Ulrich Thürauf,
vol. 65, 1924 (Munich, 1927), p. 397; Stresemann, Vermächtnis, I, 315-316.
Article 213 of the Treaty of Versailles said: "So long as the present Treaty
remains in force, Germany undertakes to give every facility for any investigation which the Council of the League of Nations, acting if need be by
a majority vote, may consider necessary."

[36] Stresemann, "Nachlass," 3111/7122/146711 ff.

to the League equivalent to the complete cessation of such control.

The Allies, in their reply on March 6, 1924, denied the validity of Stresemann's arguments and insisted on their right to continue full military control in all fields, not merely those singled out in the five points. Before any concessions in this respect could be made, they wanted a final general inspection, to make certain that Germany had actually completed her disarmament (except for the five points). Once this general inspection had been satisfactorily completed and the settlement of the controversial five points seemed assured, then the withdrawal of the Control Commission and substitution of League control could be considered.[37]

The German answer on March 31 merely repeated the allegations of Stresemann's January note and contested the Allied demand for a general inspection, insisting again that German disarmament, except for the five points, had been completed. If the Allies had any doubts on this score, they should request the Council of the League to make any investigations it felt necessary. The League, the German note stated, would act not merely in the interest of a few powers, but of Europe as a whole; and what was even more important, it might consider the disarmament of Germany as part of general disarmament, to show that the object of its investigation was not "to maintain permanently the disproportion now existing between the state of German armament and that of Germany's neighbors, but the loyal and final pacification of Europe."[38]

While this tug-of-war between the German Foreign Office and the Allied Conference of Ambassadors over a general military inspection was going on, the Allied control officers were

[37] Schulthess, vol. 65 (1924), pp. 399-400; Macartney, Survey of International Affairs 1925 (II), pp. 174-175.
[38] Schulthess, vol. 65 (1924), pp. 400-402; Macartney, Survey of International Affairs 1925 (II), pp. 175-176.

finding their task made more difficult by hostile demonstrations on the part of the German populace, a fact which Stresemann still hoped might help to stop the control visits.[39] The man who more than anyone else was concerned over these visits was Seeckt. But instead of recognizing the efforts made in the army's behalf by Stresemann, the general merely added to the Foreign Minister's worries. The latter's argument that German obstinacy in military matters might have harmful repercussions in the realm of foreign relations was impatiently brushed aside by the head of the Reichswehr.[40] Seeckt, for obvious reasons, was especially interested in keeping Allied control missions away from his army units and installations, and he refused categorically to issue the necessary orders to facilitate their work.[41] He did not agree, moreover, with Stresemann's contention that the shift of control from Allied Commission to League Council would ease matters for Germany—on the contrary, French influence in the League would result in still stricter supervision. The controversy between the two over the future control functions of the League, according to Rabenau, became so violent that some people felt Stresemann might use this issue to overthrow Seeckt.[42] Actually Stresemann appears to have shown the greater patience in these internal wranglings. In a letter to Reichswehrminister Gessler, with whom he was on much better terms, he expressed the hope that any friction between their respective ministries could be avoided, "since we shall probably be dependent for some time on furthering, through collaboration in mutual trust, the interests of the Reich in these difficult times."[43]

The conflict between Seeckt and Stresemann reached a high

---

[39] Stresemann, *Vermächtnis*, I, 316; Stresemann, "Nachlass," 3106/7167/155423.
[40] Rabenau, *Seeckt*, p. 394.
[41] Stresemann, "Nachlass," 3111/7122/146618.
[42] Rabenau, *Seeckt*, p. 407.
[43] Stresemann, "Nachlass," 3118/7171/156240.

point in June 1924, after the Allies had made clear their firm stand in the matter of military control. In reply to the German proposals of March 31, the Allied Conference of Ambassadors at Paris, on May 28, presented the German government with the alternatives of either agreeing to the proposed general inspection, followed (if its results proved satisfactory) by a considerable reduction of Allied control organs; or else facing "the strict application of the Treaty," i. e., continuation of full-scale Allied control until all terms of the Treaty had been fully complied with. Germany was asked to reply to this Allied proposal not later than June 30.[44]

Shortly after this ultimatum-like note had been delivered, a general election in France brought the resignation of Poincaré from the premiership and the rise in his place of Herriot. As one of his first acts the new Premier visited Britain's Prime Minister Ramsay MacDonald; and since there had been rumors to the effect that Germany might turn down the Allied note, the two Prime Ministers, on June 24, addressed an urgent request to the Germans, asking for a favorable reply. They expressed concern over the "continued and increasing activities of nationalist and militarist associations, which are more or less openly organizing military forces to precipitate further armed conflict in Europe," and begged the German government to aid "in giving effect to the legitimate requirements of the Military Commission of Control." "So soon as the several points on which the Allied Governments have explained that they must be satisfied shall have been properly met," they added, "the Allied Governments are ready and anxious to see the machinery of the Control Commission replaced by the rights of investigation conferred on the Council of the League of Nations by Article 213 of the Treaty."[45]

[44] *Schulthess*, vol. 65 (1924), pp. 410-411; Macartney, *Survey of International Affairs 1925* (II), p. 176.

[45] Stresemann, "Nachlass," 3117/7170/156023 ff. MacDonald had already

This certainly was by far the most conciliatory statement made thus far by the Allies on German military control. But it did not elicit a similarly cordial reply, despite Lord D'Abernon's warning to the German government "that the tone of their reply was a matter of supreme importance—that they had an opportunity to alter the whole atmosphere of their foreign relations. . . ." [46] While the cabinet as a whole realized that the time had come when Germany could no longer evade the issue of one last general control visit, Seeckt (who only had "an advisory voice" in the deliberations) remained opposed to any kind of further control.[47] Some fifty-one different drafts, it was rumored, were submitted for discussion, before Stresemann himself finally produced the one that was generally acceptable.[48] To satisfy Seeckt, it stated that the methods of inspection to be adopted should be decided by negotiations between the Allies and Germany. Seeckt was assured, furthermore, that the army would be given a hand in these negotiations and that Germany would insist that control activities be concentrated primarily against factories rather than against the army itself. If Allied officers should try to visit army installations, Secretary of State von Schubert told Lord D'Abernon, "that would be the end"; and Stresemann himself issued a similar warning to Italy's ambassador Bosdari.[49] But as usual the army did not recognize these efforts in its behalf, even though, in the course of July, it was actually given the leading role in negotiating with the Allied Control Commission, the Foreign Office stepping down into

urged Stresemann on June 1 not to turn down the Allied note since it opened the way to an early termination of military control: *ibid.*, 3117/7169/155847.

[46] D'Abernon, *Diary*, III, *Dawes to Locarno 1924-1926* (New York, 1931), p. 76.

[47] Rabenau, *Seeckt*, p. 403.

[48] D'Abernon, *Diary*, III, 77.

[49] Stresemann, "Nachlass," 3112/7127/147601, 147638; *ibid.*, 3118/7171/156254.

second place.[50] "Our struggle," a Reichswehr memorandum
stated, "was not directed so much against France but against the
Foreign Office. . . . As long as Reichswehr and Foreign Office
do not pull in one direction, namely in the direction of military
preparedness (*Wehrhaftmachung*) of the people, things will not
go any better in foreign and domestic affairs."[51] In a similar
vein Rabenau states that "the successful resistance [to Allied
military control] originated entirely, solely, and clearly with
Seeckt, in opposition to the Foreign Office and possibly even to
its minister, i. e., Stresemann."[52]

As far as Stresemann was concerned, these judgments were
much too loose. His frequent quarrels with Seeckt did not arise
because of any basic divergence of views on the necessity of
German rearmament. On several occasions Stresemann actually
regretted the lack of a strong army as "the main factor in a
successful foreign policy."[53] What he objected to was the well-
nigh unassailable position which Seeckt and his Reichswehr
had cut out for themselves within the Weimar Republic, a
position which posed a constant threat to that "primacy of
foreign policy" which was one of Stresemann's basic tenets. The
ideal solution to him would have been the reintroduction of
universal military service, which not only would have restored
Germany's military might, but would at the same time have done
away with Seeckt's *Söldnerheer*. To make such a move palatable
to the Allies, Stresemann (in early 1924) thought of stressing
the advantages of a large and loyal republican army as opposed
to the small and highly selective Reichswehr, whose ranks had
become "estranged" from the German people. Not only would
such a "citizens' army" be useful in putting down domestic

[50] *Ibid.*, 3118/7171/156236 ff.
[51] Germany, Heeresarchiv Potsdam, "Papers of General Hans von Seeckt,"
Roll 21 (June 1924).
[52] Rabenau, *Seeckt*, p. 452.
[53] Stresemann, "Nachlass," 3120/7180/157925; *ibid.*, 3097/7113/145099 ff.

disturbances, but it would also avert the danger of a dictatorship, which Seeckt and his Reichswehr might set up whenever they chose.[54] While these schemes were never openly broached to the Allies, they certainly show that Stresemann was as much interested in the *Wehrhaftmachung* of the German people as any other German patriot.

The German reply to the Allied note of May 28 and to the Herriot–MacDonald letter of June 24 was delivered on June 30. Its general tone was one of hurt innocence, and D'Abernon's apprehension, before he even saw it, that there was "a strong tendency in the German mind to start every memorandum with a series of conditions and reserves" proved well-founded.[55] Most of the "nationalist and militarist associations" over which Herriot and MacDonald had shown such concern were presented as mere "sporting and athletic organizations," that fulfilled the educational (as distinguished from military) functions formerly performed by universal military service. As for the few actual political organizations, the German government had made "serious endeavors" to carry out their disarmament, so there could be "no question of these associations being really armed." There was, the note continued, a "deep feeling of bitterness among the German people concerning the present situation" and a failure to understand how anyone could seriously think that Germany, so completely disarmed, was a threat to the peace of Europe. German public opinion "revolted against renewed Inter-Allied control" as "an infringement of the sovereignty of the Reich which, besides being in itself very humiliating indeed, appears no longer to be authorized by the Treaty of Versailles." Still— in view of the general trend towards conciliation, the German

---

[54] *Ibid.*, 3106/7167/155386; Rabenau, *Seeckt*, p. 408. At the same time such an army would also avoid the opposite extreme of a Socialist militia, which Stresemann had feared during the early postwar years: Schlottner, *Stresemann*, pp. 37, 44.

[55] D'Abernon, *Diary*, III, 77.

government declared itself ready to make the heavy sacrifice of permitting a general inspection "on the basis of the express declaration of the Allied Governments that the general inspection demanded means the conclusion of Inter-Allied Military Control and transition to the procedure contemplated under Article 213 of the Peace Treaty." Also, as already pointed out, the German note insisted that the methods of this general inspection should be decided in negotiations between the Allies and Germany; and finally it requested that such inspection be concluded by September 30, 1924.[56]

It took the Allies little more than a week to respond to Germany's acceptance of a general inspection by the Inter-Allied Commission. They pointed out, however, that this general inspection did not affect the continuation of military control until the controversial five points had been cleared up as well. As to the duration of the general inspection, the Allies refused to set a final date, but promised to expedite matters and to begin control operations on July 20. This Allied refusal to consider the conditions which Germany had attached to her acceptance evoked an outcry from German nationalists and their demand, in an open letter to Stresemann, that the Allied note be rejected. But the German government decided to co-operate, so that after more than six months of negotiations, the Allies at last seemed to have gained their point.[57]

The actual inspection did not begin until September 8, and in the first six weeks close to eight hundred control visits were carried out.[58] At the start things went quite smoothly; but beginning in November, several difficulties arose: there were the first outbreaks of mob violence against Allied officers;[59] there

[56] *Schulthess*, vol. 65 (1924), pp. 413-415; Macartney, *Survey of International Affairs 1925 (II)*, pp. 177-178.

[57] *Schulthess*, vol. 65 (1924), p. 418; Macartney, *Survey of International Affairs 1925 (II)*, pp. 178-179.

[58] Macartney, *Survey of International Affairs 1925 (II)*, pp. 179-182.

[59] Stresemann, "Nachlass," 3120/7179/157755 ff.

were rumors (supported by facts) in the French and British press to the effect that German disarmament was by no means as complete as had been asserted by the German government;[60] and finally, there was passive opposition on the part of the Reichswehr, which together with the Foreign Office was "assisting" the Control Commission in its task.[61]

At the same time an early and successful conclusion of control operations gained added significance in connection with Article 429 of the Versailles Treaty. This article provided that if Germany lived up to her obligations under the Treaty, the northernmost zone of the Rhineland (which was to be occupied for fifteen years as a guarantee for the execution of the treaty) might be evacuated after only five years, i. e., on January 10, 1925. Throughout the summer of 1924, both MacDonald and Herriot had dropped repeated hints that such evacuation would depend on Germany's living up to the disarmament terms of Versailles.[62] An official statement that the evacuation, which the Germans still took for granted, might not be forthcoming, was made by Lord Curzon in the House of Lords on December 18. Because of "constant and persistent obstruction from German hands," Curzon stated, the report of the Allied Control Commission had been delayed, and only after it had been received and duly examined, could any decision about the Rhineland be made. The Commission did, however, hand in a preliminary report, and on its basis the Conference of Ambassadors, on December 28, decided to postpone the evacuation. The German government was officially notified of this decision on January 5, 1925. The Allied note, while not going into great detail, did mention a number of specific points on which Germany had defaulted: reconstruction, in different form, of the Great General

[60] *Ibid.*, 3119/7176/157003.
[61] *Ibid.*, 3119/7175/156819-20.
[62] *Ibid.*, 3118/7172/156422; *ibid.*, 3118/7173/156623 ff.; *ibid.*, 3119/7176/156899.

Staff; short-term recruitment and training of volunteers; failure
to convert armament works to civilian production; retention of
excess military equipment; failure to reorganize the police; and
failure to adopt the governmental measures demanded by the
Allies on September 29, 1922. i.e., prohibition of export and
import of war material, and adjustment of Reichswehr recruiting and organization to the terms of the Versailles Treaty.[63]

The German reaction to this Allied move was stunned indignation. On December 20, two weeks before the Allied objections were officially communicated to the German government,
the cabinet met and tried to chart its course. There had been
a good deal of concern, outwardly at least, that Allied failure to
evacuate the northern Rhineland might lead to outbursts of
protest among rightist circles against Stresemann's policy. It is
surprising, therefore, to find the Foreign Minister stating at the
outset that "theoretically the fight for evacuation by January 10
must be carried on with all possible energy, even though actually
a postponement of the evacuation until May is bearable, if simultaneously the evacuation of the Ruhr will take place." "The
Control Commission," Stresemann continued, "will say that
some matters of disarmament have not been complied with,"
especially the concentration of large numbers of police in army
barracks. These units, he suggested, might be diminished, but
not abolished. Minister of Defense Gessler branded the whole
matter as a "political maneuver of the Entente," but recognized
the danger that "German public opinion, believing Curzon's
statements, might attack us [i.e., the government]." [64] The most
tantalizing aspect of the whole affair seems to have been that
prior to January 5 nobody really knew what specific points the
Allies would raise in their note. In view of such uncertainty, the
strategy of belittling what could not be denied had to serve its

[63] *Schulthess*, vol. 66 (1925), p. 399.
[64] Stresemann, "Nachlass," 3111/7125/147227 ff.; *ibid.*, 3120/7179/
157832.

purpose again. "Even if the reproaches levelled against us in the matter of disarmament were true," Stresemann told the foreign press on December 30, "which has been denied by the declarations of the Reichswehrminister in the *Berliner Tageblatt*, what difference would 20 or even 100,000 rifles make in the fact that Germany is actually disarmed?" (The difference, someone might have pointed out, that Germany's past protestations of disarmament had been proved untrue!) And he went on to make the startling announcement that there were years when "Germany could not even fill the army contingent of 100,000 men she was entitled to under the peace treaty, since nobody could be found any more who wanted to sign up for twelve years." [65]

After the note of January 5 had been received, Stresemann, in his immediate reply, objected to its vagueness which made any German rejoinder impossible. As soon as more details were presented, he said, the German government would answer them point by point. To justify the delay in evacuating the northern Rhineland zone, however, by the incomplete state of German disarmament was, in his opinion, a mistake. Given the military weakness of Germany, a few violations, if they actually existed, could not possibly deserve such harsh punishment.[66] "I have no doubt," Stresemann advised Konrad Adenauer, then Lord Mayor of Cologne, "that the detailed report of the Allies will mention a whole series of so-called defaults which, in their individual claims, cannot perhaps be simply rejected. I should recommend, therefore, not to enter into any discussion of these alleged defaults." [67] Despite such careful adjectives as "so-called"

[65] Stresemann, *Vermächtnis*, I, 620. Stresemann, "Nachlass," 3120/7179/157846. See also Stresemann's report to the Reichstag's Foreign Affairs Committee: *ibid.*, 3120/7180/157884 ff.

[66] *Schulthess*, vol. 66 (1925), pp. 399-401; Stresemann, *Vermächtnis*, II, 23-24.

[67] Stresemann, "Nachlass," 3120/7180/157905.

and "alleged," one senses a certain apprehension of what the
final report of the Control Commission might contain. There
was a further exchange of notes on January 26-27: Germany
again registered indignation at the Allied note of January 5,
and the Allies, in reply, reiterated their decision not to evacuate
the Rhineland at this time.[68]

The report of the Inter-Allied Control Commission was
actually completed on February 15.[69] But it took almost four
months before the Conference of Ambassadors could agree on
the text of the note to be delivered to the Germans. During
these months the center of the diplomatic stage was taken over
by the preliminary negotiations which ultimately were to lead
to the Locarno Pact, with its spectacular lessening of Allied-
German tension.[70] Part of the delay in the drafting of the disarmament note was due to a growing divergence of views between France and Great Britain on the question of security,
with the latter taking Germany's failure to live up to her
disarmament obligations a good deal more lightly than the
former. "Personally I have no doubt whatever," D'Abernon
wrote in early January, "that any danger from German military
organisations has long since ceased to exist."[71] But this view
was not shared by the French. "Our establishment on the
Rhine," Herriot said on January 28, "is the essential and, alas,
the last condition of our security. . . . Remember that France
has constantly had to discuss peace with a dagger an inch off
her heart. Let us away with this dagger."[72]

[68] *Schulthess*, vol. 66 (1925), pp. 401-402; Macartney, *Survey of Inter-national Affairs 1925 (II)*, pp. 183-185.
[69] A hint of what the report contained was given to the Germans by Italy's ambassador Bosdari on February 26: Stresemann, "Nachlass," 3114/7135/148912 ff.
[70] Macartney, *Survey of International Affairs 1925 (II)*, pp. 17 ff.; Bretton, *Stresemann*, pp. 86 ff.
[71] D'Abernon, *Diary*, III, 120-121.
[72] Macartney, *Survey of International Affairs 1925 (II)*, p. 15. In order

Finally, on June 5, 1925, after lengthy inter-Allied negotiations, the disarmament note was presented to the Germans. It
was an extensive document and in its effect a formidable indict-
ment of Germany's failure to disarm. This failure, it said,
"would in the aggregate enable the German government eventu-
ally to reconstitute an army modeled on the principle of a nation
in arms."[73] In considerable detail the note spelled out the various points on which the Control Commission in its report had
found Germany to be in default: the excessive size and military
character of her police force; her failure to convert industrial
production in specific factories to nonmilitary purposes, the
stock-piling of excess weapons and strategic materials; revival,
in the guise of the *Heeresleitung* (more correctly the *Truppenamt*), of the prewar General Staff; use of civilian aircraft
for military purposes; military training in arms not authorized
by the Peace Treaty; short-term enlistment of volunteers and
military activities of rightist organizations—these are only some
of the more important points, many of which, as we have seen,
had already played a role in earlier exchanges between the Allies
and Germany.

The actual report of the Control Commission was not officially
brought to the attention of the German government, but the
French, on June 8, published extensive excerpts from it in the
Paris press.[74] These told of the unending series of obstacles
which the Commission had encountered in its dealings with the
German military and, in staggering detail, gave the many instances of secret rearmament which the control officers had been

not to increase these French fears, Stresemann, in March of 1925, strongly
objected to the possible candidacy of Reichswehrminister Gessler for the
presidency of the Reich, after Ebert's death: Stresemann, "Nachlass," 3166/
7310/158433 ff.

[73] For its text see Great Britain, Foreign Office, Germany No. 2 (1925),
*Note Presented to the German Government by the British, French, Italian,
Japanese and Belgian Ambassadors at Berlin*, Command Paper 2429.

[74] *Schulthess*, vol. 66 (1925), pp. 404-408.

able to uncover despite German obstructions. German industry, the report stated, was still in a position "to produce quickly and in large masses the war material which the country was lacking." The Reichswehr was pictured as an "army of cadres," which could draw on large reserves from short-term volunteers, auxiliary police, and patriotic organizations. The report did not deal in mere generalizations but singled out specific factories and the quantities and types of military stores that had been discovered in them. It gave the names of places where members of civilian patriotic organizations had been given military training by the armed forces and on what dates. And it accused the German government, not just the army, of complicity in these illegal activities. "The German authorities," the report stated, "did everything possible to hide the existence and activities of these patriotic organizations." "It is significant," it said, "that the authors of certain newspaper articles revealing violations of the treaty have been accused and prosecuted for high treason and given heavy sentences, while organizations engaging in activities that violated the terms of the treaty, have been treated with leniency by the authorities."

The importance of the Control Commission's report lies not so much in the detailed enumeration of German disarmament violations, impressive as that was, but in its emphasis on the inherent potentialities of German industry to produce war material in large quantities and the equally important capabilities of the Reichswehr as a *Führerheer*, an army of potential leaders for a future mass army. Compared to the individual breaches of the Versailles disarmament terms, these general considerations, as later events were to prove, were of basic significance. Unfortunately, however, Allied-German negotiations came to be concentrated almost exclusively on individual points. And with Germany's readiness to meet Allied demands on these detailed violations the underlying threat of German industry and Reichswehr to expand was gradually lost sight of.

The detailed charges made in the Allied note of June 5 and the report of the Control Commission on which this note was based came at a time when Stresemann had embarked on the major diplomatic effort of his career: the negotiations for a western security pact, which was signed at Locarno on October 16, 1925. We cannot here go into all the motives that led each of the participants to conclude such a pact. In the case of Germany these included the desire to liberate her western provinces from the "stranglehold" of Allied occupation (as Stresemann put it), and to calm French fears on the subject of German rearmament. A "top secret" memorandum among Stresemann's unpublished papers, dated February 9, 1925, makes this quite clear. "The presently acute questions of disarmament and evacuation," it states, "are often judged in France from the point of view of security against possible German plans for aggression. They could thus probably be solved more easily if they were tied in with a general agreement securing the peace between Germany and France." [75] Such an agreement was concluded at Locarno. Its effect, as is generally known, was to usher in a brief era of good feeling between Germany and the West, an era which, to the present day, evokes nostalgia in those who lived through it. And the men responsible for giving the world this glimpse of a more reasonable approach to the settlement of international differences—the Frenchman Aristide Briand, the Englishman Austen Chamberlain, and the German Gustav Stresemann—were rewarded for their efforts in 1926 with the Nobel Peace Prize.

We are here concerned chiefly with the German member of this trio. In the light of what happened in Germany after 1933, some people began to wonder whether the general confidence in the idealism and peacefulness of Stresemann's ultimate aims had not perhaps been misplaced. And turning to the published

---

[75] Stresemann, "Nachlass," 3166/7309/158121; see also *ibid.*, 3165/7415/175571-72.

excerpts from his papers, the three volumes of the *Vermächtnis*, they found a few items that seemed to bear out their doubts.[76] Most prominent among these were the famous letter Stresemann had written in September 1925 to the former German Crown Prince, in which he used Metternich's term *"finassieren"* to describe the short-range aims of his policy,[77] and the somewhat earlier letter to von Maltzan (then ambassador in Washington), in which the Foreign Minister pointed out that his security pact would "protect the Rhineland from the consequences of France's policy of persecution, split the Entente, and open new possibilities in the East."[78] This is not the place to re-examine the long-range goals of Stresemann's foreign policy. Some insight into this question can be gained from the rich material of his unpublished papers. Though the Foreign Minister, as he told the Crown Prince, felt that at all times he had to observe "great restraint" in his utterances, so the last word on the subject will have to wait until the documents of the German Foreign Office for the Weimar period are made accessible to scholars. The present inquiry into Stresemann's position on the question of German rearmament during these crucial months, I think, will show the necessity for such a re-examination.

Considering the comprehensive and detailed nature of the Allied charges, one might have expected indignation, concern, or at least surprise on Stresemann's part about the activities of the Reichswehr which so completely ran counter to the professed aims of his foreign policy. But the Foreign Minister showed none of these reactions. On the contrary—the Allied note, he felt, was

[76] For examples of this critical approach see Godfrey Scheele, *The Weimar Republic* (London, 1946), pp. 232 ff.; George Boas, "Stresemann: Object Lesson in Post-War Leadership," *Public Opinion Quarterly*, VIII (1944), 232-243; see also Lionel Kochan, "Stresemann and the Historians," *The Wiener Library Bulletin*, VII, No. 5-6 (September-December 1953), p. 35.

[77] Stresemann, *Vermächtnis*, II, 553-555. For a complete version of the letter see Stresemann, "Nachlass," 3168/7318/159871 ff.

[78] Stresemann, *Vermächtnis*, II, 281-282.

"sadistic, especially in its demand for the destruction of war
material," a "complete *Geheimratsarbeit* [work of bureaucrats],
devoid of bold lines."[79] In a cabinet meeting, which was convened immediately on June 5, he referred to the Allied charges
as "pitiful and petty." "There is nothing in the Treaty of
Versailles," Stresemann said, "which holds that we cannot further develop our Reichswehr in case of an attack"; to which
Gessler added that if Germany should again run into a critical
domestic situation, she must "as she had already done twice
before, knowingly and on purpose violate the terms of the
Treaty." Hindenburg, who just recently had become President,
conducted the meeting, but did not participate in the debate.[80]
In discussions outside the closed doors of the cabinet and in
public utterances, Stresemann ridiculed "the legend of an
aggressive Germany, bristling with arms,"[81] and took issue with
some of the specific points raised by the Allies. He was particularly stirred up over any further dismantling of German factories,
which, as far back as January 1925, he had branded as British
maneuvers to kill German competition.[82] He told the American
and Italian ambassadors that the destruction of some of Krupp's
equipment would interfere with German production for export
and hence inhibit the fulfillment of Germany's obligations under
the Dawes Plan.[83] Stresemann repeated the same argument at a
luncheon with some members of the Inter-Allied Control Commission. But Britain's General Wauchope, who was present, told
him that the Allies were not really interested in destruction but
rather in dispersal of machinery.[84] This, the Foreign Minister
felt, was a valuable bit of information, so he immediately handed

[79] Stresemann, "Nachlass," 3113/7129/147837.
[80] *Ibid.*, 3114/7133/148794 ff.
[81] *Ibid.*, 3114/7133/148805-806.
[82] *Ibid.*, 3120/7180/157884 ff.
[83] Stresemann, *Vermächtnis*, II, 260-261; Stresemann, "Nachlass," 3111/
7122/147190.
[84] Stresemann, "Nachlass," 3143/7314/159168.

it on to Krupp von Bohlen.[85] We now know, from Krupp's own statements, that beginning in 1922, his firm began to collaborate with the Reichswehr "to keep his shops and personnel in readiness, if the occasion should arise, for armament orders later on," and that some of the basic principles of design for such forbidden weapons as tanks had been worked out as early as 1926.[86] What we do not know is how far Stresemann was informed of the details of these arrangements. Of their general existence, however, he cannot have been unaware. In November 1925, Seeckt paid a four-day visit to the Ruhr, inspecting its industries and discussing questions of rearmament with a large number of prominent industrialists, several of them members of Stresemann's party. There could be no doubt in anyone's mind about the purpose of such a visit.[87] Another point in the Allied note which aroused the Foreign Minister's criticism was its objection to the size of Germany's police and the concentration of some of its units in barracks. The police, he claimed, was needed to put down communist uprisings; and in order to facilitate quick mobilization, they had to be housed in barracks.[88]

But no matter how much Stresemann took the army's side in its controversy with the Allies over disarmament, General von Seeckt did not repay in kind by supporting Stresemann's foreign policy. On the contrary, he came out flatly against the "comedy" of Locarno, which he opposed "by all possible means." As Mrs. von Seeckt put it at a dinner party: "Nothing will come of Locarno, my husband won't tolerate it." [89] "The ugly point in

[85] *Ibid.*, 3143/7314/159173, 159179.
[86] Germany, U. S. Zone of Occupation, Military Tribunals, *Trials of War Criminals*, IX, 263 ff.; *ibid.*, X, 426.
[87] *Ibid.*, X, 422 ff.
[88] Stresemann, "Nachlass," 3143/7314/159168; Stresemann, *Vermächtnis*, II, 33. On the military significance of the police for the rearmament of Germany under Hitler, see Taylor, *Sword and Swastika*, p. 31.
[89] Stresemann, "Nachlass," 3100/7140/149756. The arrogance of the

the center of the whole problem," Seeckt wrote in early July, "is of course Herr Str[esemann]. . . . One doesn't like to change jockeys during a race, but the question remains whether it is not more important at long last to get rid of this man and thus clear the way for a different foreign policy."[90] The reasons for Seeckt's hostile attitude, besides a general dislike for the author of Locarno, were his aversion to France and his opposition to Germany's joining the League of Nations. The ultimate shift of military supervision to that body, which Stresemann envisaged, would simply mean a perpetuation of such supervision.[91] The General was unaware or unwilling to admit the obvious military advantages of the Locarno Pact. Besides relieving Allied-German tension, a factor which by itself was to prove most advantageous to the Reichswehr's undercover activities, it also enabled Germany to concentrate most of her military planning against the East, where the threat of a clash with Poland was seen as a constant possibility.[92] It was only through Gessler's support of Stresemann's Locarno policy that Seeckt's opposition became somehow neutralized.[93] As far as Germany's entry into the League was concerned, the argument that seems to have finally overcome Seeckt's reluctance was that "if one wanted to ruin an organization or club, it was always better to be a member rather than learn only by hearsay what was going on inside."[94]

The feeling of good will that was generated as the negotiations for a security pact progressed made itself felt as early as the summer of 1925 and quite naturally helped to soothe the irritation that had arisen earlier during the year over Germany's failure to live up to her disarmament obligations. The Germans

statement is somewhat lost in translation: "Aus Locarno wird nichts, das duldet mein Mann nicht." See also *ibid.*, 3113/7129/147935.

[90] Rabenau, *Seeckt*, pp. 406, 418-419.
[91] Stresemann, "Nachlass," 3113/7129/147935; *ibid.*, 3113/7131/148245 ff.
[92] Rabenau, *Seeckt*, p. 423; Görlitz, *Generalstab*, p. 358.
[93] Bernhard, "Seeckt und Stresemann," p. 471.
[94] Rabenau, *Seeckt*, p. 408.

continued to quibble over some of the points raised in the note
of June 5, but nevertheless declared their willingness to expedite
the settlement of those Allied objections they felt were justified.[95]
In July the Reichswehr Ministry appointed a special commission
under Major-General von Pawelsz to collaborate with the Allied
Control Commission in carrying out "what the Allies had a right
to demand under the Versailles Treaty."[96] In October it was
announced that Krupp at long last had begun demolishing its
gun-making plant. And even French political and military
leaders now began to admit that Germany was taking satisfactory
steps toward disarmament.[97]

There was no official German reply to the note of June 5
until after Locarno. But as was to be expected, and as Stresemann had hoped,[98] the topic of German disarmament came up
on several occasions during that conference. Thus far, the offensive in this matter had rested almost exclusively with the Allies,
who had accused Germany of violating the terms of Versailles
and had left Stresemann to deny or explain away these violations.
But as Germany gradually regained a status of equality among
the great powers, she began to inject a new argument into the
discussion by attacking the general principle of unilateral German disarmament itself. With German membership in the
League of Nations merely a question of time, Germany's future
obligations under Article 16 of the League Covenant served as
a convenient opening to advance this argument. "As long as
the present inequality of armaments, caused by the disarmament
of Germany, persists," Stresemann had said back in December
1924, "Germany will be unable, unlike other members of the
League of Nations, to participate in any League action under
Article 16. A disarmed people, surrounded by well-armed

[95] Stresemann, *Vermächtnis*, II, 265.
[96] *Ibid.*, II, 157.
[97] Macartney, *Survey of International Affairs 1925 (II)*, p. 190.
[98] Stresemann, "Nachlass," 3166/7311/158482.

neighbors, . . . which does not have the means to defend its borders against these forces, cannot afford to give up its neutrality without further consideration." [99] At Locarno, the Foreign Minister spoke still more plainly. In an oratorical duel with Briand, he accused the Allies of having "carried the whole principle of disarmament against Germany too far," and blamed them for conditions in which Germany could not render the aid they expected from her under Article 16. It was doubtful, he said, if Germany, in case of a Russian attack, had sufficient forces even to put down the upheavals of pro-Russian elements inside Germany. And he pointed to the contradiction between Allied insistence that the Reichswehr be merely a border-police and their demand for military aid from such a police force in case of war. "I ask Herr Briand," he concluded, "to stick to the facts as they are and as they have come to be not through Germany's will, but against the will of Germany." [100] What Stresemann was aiming at was equality of armaments (or disarmament) among the powers. "We expect," he said during the famous cruise aboard the *Orange Blossom*, "that the League of Nations . . . introduce a general disarmament which will include a minimum of troops for each state, but a relatively equal minimum." [101]

This demand, as is well known, was to remain a subject of fruitless international discussions for years to come. It derived added moral justification, in German eyes at least, from the preamble to Part V of the Versailles Treaty. [102] One of the important long-range effects of this German insistence on general disarmament was to undermine the hitherto self-assertive stand

[99] Quoted in Bretton, *Stresemann*, p. 140.

[100] Stresemann, *Vermächtnis*, II, 191-192.

[101] *Ibid.*, II, 193. See also Stresemann's "Richtlinien für Locarno." Stresemann, "Nachlass," 3113/7129/147969 ff.

[102] The preamble for Part V stated: "In order to render possible the initiation of a general limitation of the armaments of all nations, Germany undertakes strictly to observe the military, naval and air clauses which follow."

the Allies had taken on German rearmament and to make them
increasingly lenient towards violations which up to now they
had castigated in the most severe terms. Already the talks at
Locarno, in so far as they touched on these violations, showed
which way developments were going. After the damning evidence which the note of June 5 had adduced, one would have
expected the usual evasions and excuses on Stresemann's part.
But far from it. "I demanded," he tells us, "35,000 policemen
quartered in barracks instead of 25,000, continuation of the
[present type of] supreme command in the Reichswehr, and
freedom in the training of our troops." And for good measure
he added: "I have no idea what your soldiers are still doing
in the occupied area [of the Rhineland]. I see no reason for
their being there, since they no longer need defend France's
security." Briand "almost fell off the sofa" when he heard this,
and expressed admiration for Stresemann's "audacity bordering
on foolhardiness," adding that, as far as Stresemann was concerned, probably "the whole Treaty of Versailles might as well
cease to exist."[103] Briand's quip was not far off the mark, as
events soon were to show.

It was actually during the talks at Locarno that the contents
of the next exchange of notes on German disarmament was
agreed upon, with Stresemann suggesting both what Germany
was to say and what the Allies were to reply. Briand and
Chamberlain agreed to this somewhat unorthodox procedure.[104]
The German note was delivered on October 23.[105] As Stresemann had indicated at Locarno, it stated that a considerable
number of the points enumerated in the last Allied note of

[103] Stresemann, "Nachlass," 3169/7319/160020 ff.
[104] Stresemann, *Vermächtnis*, II, 201.
[105] For its text and the text of the Allied replies on November 6, 14, and 16,
see Great Britain, Foreign Office, *Correspondence between the Ambassadors'
Conference and the German Ambassador at Paris respecting German Disarmament, etc.*, Miscellaneous No. 12 (1925), Command Paper 2527 (London,
1925).

June 5 had by now been fulfilled and that the great majority of the remaining demands, with a few exceptions, would be settled by November 15. There were some questions, however, that presented "special difficulties" and hence required further discussion.[106] Two of these were of particular importance: the police and the General Staff.[107] The German government, the note said, desired to enlist its police for short-term service and demanded the right to keep 35,000 of its members in military formations, quartered in barracks. With regard to the General Staff, Germany promised to reduce the number of staff officers, abolish the distinction between staff and ordinary officers, and place their appointment in the hands of the Defense Minister rather than the army command.

The Allied reply to this German note arrived on November 6 and again followed the outline Stresemann had proposed at Locarno. The Allies were "happy to note the effort made by the German Government to conform to the demands made by the Allied Governments in their note of June 5," and hoped that sufficient progress would be made on the few remaining questions so that December 1 could be fixed as the date for the evacuation of the northern Rhineland. The Allies insisted, however, "that any proposal submitted to them concerning the police must have the effect of depriving it of the nature of a military organization; and as regards associations, irrespective of their nature, the proposals must be such as shall prevent them from occupying themselves with military matters and from having any connection with the Ministry of the Reichswehr or with any other military authority. Similarly, as regards the . . . High Command, the solution to be reached must have the effect of forbidding

[106] *Ibid.*, p. 5. These were: (1) Police (titles of higher officials, rules for personnel, barracks); (2) High Command; (3) Prohibition of training with certain weapons; (4) Artillery arming of the fortress of Königsberg; (5) Associations.

[107] Macartney, *Survey of International Affairs 1925 (II)*, pp. 190-191.

the maintenance or the establishment of commands higher than those of army corps."[108]

These Allied conditions came as a "strong disappointment" to the Germans. The issue behind this post-Locarno exchange of notes was in reality not so much the question of disarmament as the Allied evacuation of the Rhineland. Such a move would give the German people tangible evidence of the advantages of the Locarno agreements, and thus would help overcome the considerable opposition which these agreements aroused, especially among rightist circles, in Germany. To erase the negative effect of the Allied note, Briand, on November 8, sent a representative to tell Stresemann that no matter what, the evacuation of the northern Rhineland would "under all circumstances begin on December 1."[109] As for disarmament, Briand hoped to transfer future discussions from military to civilian hands, where agreement would be easier than among military experts. The Allies were willing furthermore, Briand's emissary stated, to make far-reaching concessions in regard to the High Command and the police. Concerning the nationalist organizations, all they expected was a declaration on the part of the German government that there was no connection between these groups and the Reichswehr, and that they did not pursue any military aims. And finally the Allies hoped that Germany would promise not to use any forbidden arms.

In the light of this conciliatory message from Briand, supplemented by similar efforts at appeasement on the part of Lord D'Abernon,[110] it is not surprising that the next German note, delivered on November 11, tried to make the most of the Allies' willingness to compromise.[111] As far as the existing organization

---

[108] See note 105 above.

[109] Stresemann, "Nachlass," 3113/7129/148026 ff.

[110] *Ibid.*, 148032, 148042.

[111] Macartney, *Survey of International Affairs 1925 (II)*, pp. 191-192. Neither *Schulthess*, vol. 66 (1925), nor the British White Paper cited in

of Germany's police was concerned, the Germans claimed it
was necessary in view of the ever-present danger of communism.
They denied that there were any relations between sporting
and other organizations and the Reichswehr and that Germany
had any forbidden arms. The only point on which a concession
was made was the High Command, where the German government said it was ready to satisfy Allied demands and subordinate
General von Seeckt to the civilian Minister of Defense. But
this the Germans themselves thought of as a "mere matter of
form" and not a fundamental change.[112]

Despite the obviously unsatisfactory nature of this German
reply, the Allies, on November 14 and 16, directed two notes
and a verbal declaration to the Germans in which they stated
that "complete agreement" had been reached on the disarmament questions still in dispute.[113] "In these circumstances, without waiting for the execution to be entirely completed," the note
of November 16 said, "the Allied Governments . . . have decided
. . . to proceed to the evacuation of the first zone of occupation
in the Rhineland. . . ." This evacuation was to start on December
1 and was to be completed during January 1926. It was hoped
that the German government in return would hasten the execution of its disarmament program, in which task it would be
helped by the Control Commission. "The Commission," the
note concluded, "whose members will at once be considerably
reduced, will be completely withdrawn as soon as it has brought
to a satisfactory conclusion the task that remains for it to
accomplish."

The first detachment of British troops left Cologne on November 30, and the evacuation of the northern Rhineland zone

note 105 above, which otherwise give the texts of all Allied-German communications at this time, gives the text of this one!

[112] Rabenau, *Seeckt*, p. 421; for a different view see Görlitz, *Generalstab*,
p. 359.

[113] See note 105 above.

was completed on schedule at midnight, January 31, 1926. By
that time, the Military Control Commission had been cut down
to a small nucleus, and its local branches, except for those in
Munich and Königsberg, had been abolished.[114] The Allies
clearly had lived up to their side of the bargain struck at
Locarno.[115] If Germany did the same, the end of military control
was close at hand.

---

[114] Macartney, *Survey of International Affairs 1925 (II)*, p. 193.

[115] Another concession promised at Locarno was granted in May of 1926,
when German civil aviation was freed from most of the restrictions of the
Versailles Treaty. Stresemann was well aware of the fact "that civilian
aviation might be converted into military aviation." Stresemann, "Nachlass,"
3170/7346/164801; *Schulthess*, vol. 67 (1926), p. 444.

The end of military control

III

Good quote

FROM WHAT HAS BEEN SAID thus far, one fact emerges quite clearly, and that is the untiring effort with which Stresemann worked for the withdrawal of the Inter-Allied Control Commission, even at a time when he was preoccupied with the larger issues of the Locarno Pact. Yet the end of Allied military control depended first and foremost upon Germany's fulfillment of her disarmament obligations under the Treaty of Versailles; and as we have seen, there was ample evidence of her efforts to evade these obligations wherever possible. As time went on, however, another way out presented itself for the liberation of the Reichswehr from the annoying and restricting inquisitiveness of Allied control officers. As Germany showed signs of correcting at least some of the violations charged in one Allied note after another, Allied politicians, as distinguished from their military colleagues, became increasingly willing to accept such partial fulfillment as an indication of Germany's readiness to live up to all of her obligations; especially as this readiness was proclaimed by a man of such obvious good will as Stresemann. The warnings of Allied military experts that German disarmament was far from complete were suddenly considered much too alarming and hence taken less and less seriously. Briand's confidence, that agreement on German disarmament might be reached more easily in negotiations between himself and Strese-

mann rather than in talks among military experts was sympto-
matic of this relaxation of Allied watchfulness towards Ger-
many.[1] Without such change in Allied attitude, it is doubtful
that illegal German rearmament could have survived the many
crises it caused in Allied-German relations.

Among the several factors responsible for this Allied change,
two stand out most clearly: the divergence of views between
France and Great Britain over the continued military danger
presented by a recently defeated Germany, and the general
alleviation of international tension due to the "Spirit of Locarno."
As for the first point—while the French viewed any resurgence
of German armed strength as a potential threat to their own
security, the British showed much greater apprehension over
the possible rise of German communism and tended to agree
with Stresemann and other Germans that a certain degree of
German armed strength was necessary to counteract this leftist
threat.[2] As Lord D'Abernon had put it, back in 1920: "I
consider the French demand for the total disarmament of all
Einwohnerwehr and similar organizations almost insane. It is
like cutting the branch of the tree on which you are sitting. The
French do not appear to understand that the military danger-
point is past and that the real danger in Germany is communist
disorder."[3]

The date of this statement shows that this Anglo-French
divergence originated long before Stresemann took any active

[1] Stresemann, *Vermächtnis*, II, 270; see also D'Abernon, *Diary*, III, 120-121,
on a similar divergence of views between the British ambassador and the
General Staff in London; and Stresemann, "Nachlass," 3112/7127/147638
on the same kind of disagreement in Italy.

[2] Jordan, *German Problem*, pp. 144-145, 148; Bretton, *Stresemann*, p. 139.
Italy, prior to Locarno, shared the more lenient British attitude towards
German rearmament: Stresemann, "Nachlass," 3111/7122/146713; *ibid.*,
3111/7124/147190; *ibid.*, 3112/7127/147638; *ibid.*, 3120/7179/157755 ff.;
ibid., 3120/7180/157887; *ibid.*, 3114/7133/148737.

[3] D'Abernon, *Diary*, I, *Versailles to Rapallo 1920-1922* (New York, 1929),
pp. 92-93.

part in shaping German foreign policy, though he early realized the existence of such divergence and its potential usefulness to Germany.[4] This was demonstrated in the second major factor that helped to bring about greater Allied leniency towards Germany's disarmament violations, the *détente* resulting from the Locarno negotiations. Here the deft hand of the German Foreign Minister did much to guide deliberations to conclusions favorable to Germany. Already during the talks leading to the conclusion of the Locarno Pact, Stresemann had been aware of the beneficial effects that such an agreement would have upon the final withdrawal of Allied military control.[5] Certainly as we enter the post-Locarno era, the willingness with which the Allies agreed to the evacuation of the Rhineland even before Germany had fulfilled all of her disarmament obligations served clear notice that a new era had begun. By the same token, any too blatant German disarmament violations from then on might again arouse Allied suspicions and thus endanger the process of revising the Versailles Treaty on which such promising beginnings had been made. The question is: what did Stresemann do to avert this danger? Did he follow Briand's lead in asserting the supremacy of the civilian over the military in an effort to remove any threat the latter might offer to the proclamations of politicians that a new day had dawned in the relations between victors and vanquished? More specifically—did he do anything to press the completion of German disarmament which the Allies had in mind when they withdrew their troops from the northern Rhineland? Or did he merely take advantage of the growing Allied leniency towards German rearmament to gain still further concessions and to get rid of the last vestiges of Allied military control over the Reichswehr? As will be seen, it was the latter course he adopted.

---

[4] See above, pp. 34-35; also Stresemann, "Nachlass," 3120/7180/157889.
[5] *Ibid.*, 3114/7133/148797 ff.; *ibid.*, 3166/7309/158121.

Stresemann certainly was aware of the touchiness of the disarmament problem at this particular time and he did everything
in his power to avoid giving fresh cause for Allied suspicion.
In February of 1926 the German government issued decrees
for the prevention of military training by the numerous paramilitary organizations and even dissolved one or two of the
minor ones; but such prohibitions had very little practical effect
and actually, in the words of General Blomberg, served as an
excellent screen for these associations and the Reichswehr to
hide their relationship from the probing of domestic and foreign
critics.[6] Along the same line of dispelling Allied fears, Stresemann asked Prussia's Minister of the Interior, Severing, to
prevent a projected demonstration of nationalist organizations
(those same groups about which Allied notes had expressed such
concern) in the Berlin Lustgarten.[7] The socialist Severing fully
understood the Foreign Minister's apprehension. On a previous
occasion he had used his influence to tone down the attempts
of patriotic groups to make the presidential induction of ex-Field
Marshal Hindenburg an occasion for nationalist demonstrations.
It would have been a " cruel comedy," he tells us in his memoirs,
" if the efforts at appeasement (*Dämpfungsversuche*) of Stresemann had been accompanied by martial music from Berlin to
the tune of 'Siegreich woll'n wir Frankreich schlagen'. . . ."[8]
Another possible source of embarrassment at this time was the
first of a whole series of trials involving the so-called " Feme"
murderers, i.e., those members of the " Black Reichswehr"
accused of killing " traitors" within their ranks and outside, who
had informed on German disarmament violations.[9] In January

---

[6] Jordan, *German Problem*, p. 144.

[7] Stresemann, *Vermächtnis*, II, 230.

[8] Severing, *Mein Lebensweg*, II, 56; Stresemann, " Nachlass," 3169/7322/
160515-16.

[9] On the " Feme" see Gumbel, " *Verräter verfallen der Feme*," *passim*;
Waite, *Vanguard of Nazism*, pp. 212-227.

1926, Gessler asked Stresemann's help in having the projected trial held behind closed doors, since any publicity connected with it might prove embarrassing to Germany's foreign policy. Stresemann "had the impression that aside from this way of looking at the matter, which was not usual for the gentlemen of the Reichswehr, other questions were involved, whose discussion would prove embarrassing to the army." But even so, he supported the army's plea, telling Prussia's Minister President Otto Braun that at a time when the abolition of inter-Allied military control was going through, such a public trial was most inconvenient to him, and might even endanger the withdrawal of Allied control altogether.[10]

While Stresemann was thus using his influence to keep anything out of the news that might arouse Allied fears about the German army, he received information from many quarters about continued illegal military activities. There were rumors that formations of the "Black Reichswehr" had been assembled at the fortress of Küstrin, not far from the Polish border, and at other places.[11] Stresemann's brother-in-law Kleefeld wrote from Upper Silesia and told of the reactivation of the Upper Silesian "border guards" (*Grenzschutz*) and of his (i.e., Kleefeld's) contributing 5,000 marks to their maintenance.[12] Reports from ambassador Brockdorff-Rantzau indicated that relations between the Reichswehr and the Red Army (on which more will be said in the next chapter) were still flourishing, that some 400,000 Russian grenades had just been delivered to Germany, and that ships carrying poison gas from Germany to Russia had been forced to make an emergency landing in Finland.[13] According to a note from Stresemann's secretary, three propaganda agencies,

[10] Stresemann, "Nachlass," 3100/7138/149449; Otto Braun, *Von Weimar zu Hitler* (New York, 1940), p. 208.
[11] Stresemann, "Nachlass," 3144/7324/160949; *ibid.*, 3100/7138/149457; *ibid.*, 3100/7140/149438.
[12] *Ibid.*, 3100/7138/149457.
[13] *Ibid.*, 3100/7137/149293.

disposing of "vast funds," had been set up at Kassel, Darmstadt, and Berlin, to deal with matters of illegal rearmament, and to disseminate pro-Russian propaganda to further Russo-German military relations. The note also mentioned meetings of reserve officers and non-coms in East Prussia, at which they were initiated into "technical innovations" by officers of the Reichswehr.[14] To be sure, there is no evidence that Stresemann was personally involved in these undercover activities. What these incidents do show, however, is that Germany was far from being disarmed, that she was continuing her violations of the Versailles disarmament clauses, and that Stresemann knew she was doing so.

There was one development, moreover, in which he took a direct hand. We have already mentioned Stresemann's correspondence with Major Pabst (or Peters, as he now called himself) over the amnesty promised to participants in the Kapp Putsch of 1920.[15] The amnesty had finally been granted in the summer of 1925,[16] but that did not end the Stresemann-Pabst relationship. Pabst had spent his years of exile in Austria building up the paramilitary Heimwehr; and because of that fact and his many Austrian contacts, he continued after 1925 to serve as a kind of special agent for Stresemann in Austria. In return for a yearly compensation of 12,000 marks, which Stresemann regularly sent to a Munich address, Pabst was ready at all times to carry out the Foreign Minister's "orders and instructions."[17] What these were we can only guess from the rather guarded statements in their extensive correspondence. Pabst's chief task seems to have been of a cultural and propagandist nature, supporting pro-Anschluss sentiment in Austria, serving as a link between Stresemann and certain Austrian politicians (notably Seipel and Steidle) and keeping the German Foreign Minister

[14] *Ibid.*, 3100/7138/149466 ff.
[15] See above, p. 7.
[16] Stresemann, "Nachlass," 3168/7317/159712.
[17] *Ibid.*, 3143/7313/158826, 158846.

informed on developments inside Austria and in the Italian South Tyrol.[18] But there are some indications that Pabst's activities went beyond the purely cultural and political sphere and involved military matters as well. In one of his letters to Stresemann, written in 1926, he refers to "instructions from the Bendlerstrasse" (i.e., the Reichswehr) and gives information on Italian military developments in the South Tyrol.[19] Because of their confidential nature, most of Pabst's reports to Stresemann were made in person and hence elude the historian.[20] In 1927 a representative of the Reichswehr, Major von Neuffer, returning from a visit to the Tyrol, told Seeckt of the Heimwehr's preparations against a possible Italian attack and of Pabst's hope that in such an eventuality "German associations" (*reichsdeutsche Verbände*) might come to Austria's aid. Pabst (Neuffer continued) had discussed the matter with Stresemann, and the latter "not only agreed to the promised financial support of five million marks, but had never withdrawn the promise of personal and material aid to the Tyrolean government."[21] This is not the place to go into Stresemann's Austrian policy, nor is there enough material here to draw a complete picture. It is known that he favored an eventual Anschluss and his correspondence with Pabst shows that he took a particular interest in the region of South Tyrol, which after the war had been ceded to Italy. Even the few references cited above, however, indicate that Stresemann's interest went further and that he was involved in

[18] *Ibid.*, 3143/7313/158827 ff. The funds for these activities were provided by the "Deutscher Schutzbund," which was in turn supported by the Ministry of the Interior. See Gumbel, "*Verräter verfallen der Feme*," p. 78.

[19] Stresemann, "Nachlass," 3143/7313/158838; for Stresemann's version of his relations with Pabst, see *ibid.*, 158873.

[20] Most of Pabst's letters to Stresemann announce his impending visits to Berlin: Stresemann, "Nachlass," 3143/7313/ *passim*.

[21] Germany, Heeresarchiv Potsdam, "Papers of General Hans von Seeckt," Roll 15 (January 1928).

Austro-German military relations as well. How far these relations went cannot be clearly ascertained on the basis of available evidence. But there can be little doubt that they violated Germany's (as well as Austria's) disarmament obligations.[22]

All this, together with Stresemann's knowledge of other illegal Reichswehr activities, we must keep in mind as we now turn to the negotiations during 1926 between the Allies and Germany. It will be remembered that the evacuation of the northern Rhineland had been carried out in the hope that Germany would reciprocate by living up to her remaining disarmament obligations. At the end of January 1926, the Inter-Allied Control Commission had enumerated the points on which the Germans were still held to be in default. In general these were the same that had troubled the Allies for months: police, the High Command, the use of certain forbidden arms, fortresses on the eastern frontier, and patriotic associations.[23] It was over these remaining questions that Allied and German representatives wrangled through most of 1926. Actually, it seems, the Germans were not in too great a hurry to settle the issue of Allied control. "We in the government are of the opinion," Stresemann wrote in late April, "that the military control (which really no longer deserves that name) would be more agreeable to us than a possible control by the League of Nations, as long as we are not ourselves members of that body, and the procedure of investigation [by the League] has not been settled in agreement with us. But one cannot say that in public!"[24]

Around the middle of July, the Inter-Allied Control Commission once again summed up its findings in two notes delivered to General von Pawelsz, who headed the German Disarmament

[22] Stresemann's confidant Escherisch likewise served as a link between the Foreign Minister and Austrian paramilitary groups: Stresemann, "Nachlass," 3148/7343/162244.

[23] Arnold J. Toynbee, *Survey of International Affairs 1927* (London, 1929), p. 88.

[24] Stresemann, "Nachlass," 3145/7326/161404.

Commission.[25] The German police force still exceeded the 150,000 men limit stipulated by the Allies, its training was considered to be semimilitary, and instead of enlistment for life it followed the twelve-year practice of the army and hence was able to accumulate trained reserves. With regard to the High Command, the Allies felt that the German government had not sufficiently changed the dominant status of General von Seeckt. They furthermore objected to the use of dummy tanks in army maneuvers, the use of light machine guns for the cavalry, and the flight-training of officers. The question of eastern fortifications continued to center around the construction of new fortified works at Königsberg. And finally, the Allies expressed their usual concern over the potential military threat of the numerous patriotic organizations.

This last question, together with the short-term enlistment of Reichswehr recruits (the so-called *Zeitfreiwillige*) was raised again in late August in a series of notes addressed to the German government by the Conference of Ambassadors. At that time Germany's impending admission to the League of Nations, which was scheduled for September 8, held the center of attention. There was considerable opposition at home to this latest fruit of Stresemann's Locarno policy, especially on the part of the above-mentioned patriotic associations. In trying to dispel Allied fears on this point, therefore, Stresemann was not merely playing the army's game, but he was also hoping to deprive his domestic critics of any added cause for opposing his foreign policy. In early August the Foreign Minister, through an intermediary, told Briand that the only two rightist organizations of any significance in Germany were the "Stahlhelm" and the "Jungdeutscher Orden."[26] The former, with about 800,000 members,

[25] For this and the following see Toynbee, *Survey of International Affairs 1927*, pp. 89-91; *Schulthess*, vol. 67 (1926), pp. 444-445.

[26] Stresemann, *Vermächtnis*, II, 464-465; see also the more complete version in Stresemann, "Nachlass," 3146/7330/162183.

Stresemann said "was on the decline, for lack of real tasks," and the latter, whose membership he estimated at around one million, was actively working for a Franco-German alliance against Soviet Russia.[27] To counterbalance these figures, Stresemann mentioned that the republican and socialist "Reichsbanner," which favored a socialist, i. e., nonaggressive foreign policy, was three or four million strong.

But these efforts at minimizing the importance of semimilitary, rightist organizations of some two million members did not really quiet French fears. Briand, in a letter to France's *chargé d'affaires* Laboulaye (who communicated his views to Stresemann) said that France was disturbed "because she saw in these organizations an army of several million who, at the right moment, would swell the forces of the Reichswehr. Hence the relationship between the army and these organizations was considered a grave danger." In reply Stresemann told Laboulaye that it "appeared very doubtful" to him that the intimate relations which Briand suspected between "Stahlhelm" and Reichswehr really existed. Gessler, he added, had told the Reichstag that he had deprived the "Stahlhelm" and other organizations of the support they had earlier received via the army from private (mostly industrial) sources. As far as the "Stahlhelm" went, its main concern now was with political rather than military questions. About the latest Allied notes on disarmament, which had just been delivered to the Germans, their tone, in Stresemann's opinion, was "purest Poincaré *Auslese*, vintage 1923." He would not have thought it possible that at a time when

[27] For different membership figures see Reginald H. Phelps, "The Crisis of the German Republic 1930-1932. Its Background and Course," Typescript at Widener Library, Harvard University (Cambridge, 1947), pp. 328-329. Stresemann, at an earlier date, had referred to the "Stahlhelm" and the "Jungdeutscher Orden" as "reasonable" (*vernünftige*) organizations, which he hoped to attract to his side: Stresemann, "Nachlass," 3099/7120/146153.

Germany was getting ready to join the League, these "old and buried stories" would again be dragged out.[28]

On September 8, Germany was officially admitted to the League, and two days later the German delegates took their seats in the Assembly. In his maiden speech, the German Foreign Minister reminded the rest of the powers that "the complete disarmament of Germany was laid down in the Treaty of Versailles as the beginning of universal disarmament," and he expressed hope that such universal disarmament might be effected.[29] It was during his presence in Geneva that Stresemann, on September 17, had the famous *déjeuner à deux* with Briand at the village inn of Thoiry, a secret meeting which seemed to open such glorious vistas of Franco-German collaboration.[30] A good part of the discussion on that occasion dealt with military questions, and it was, as Stresemann assures us, "not the easiest part." It was regrettable, Stresemann broached the touchy subject, that French Foreign Office representatives still found certain minor aspects of German disarmament unsettled. "One really should take this matter out of the hands of the bureaucrats (*Geheimräte*)," he added, "and simply put an end to the whole affair." Briand agreed that the question should be treated more generously. "When I first started working for the elimination of military control," he said, "the French War Ministry presented me with heavy folders of documents on German violations. I flung these folders into a corner and asked to be told the larger issues that still had to be settled, since I had no intention of bothering with such petty detail. Thereupon I was

[28] *Ibid.*, 3146/7331/162330 ff.

[29] Stresemann, *Vermächtnis*, II, 593-594.

[30] The following account is based on Stresemann, "Nachlass," 3146/7332/162515 ff., which (especially as far as German disarmament and Allied military control is concerned) is considerably more complete than the account in Stresemann, *Vermächtnis*, III, 15 ff. See also the French version in Georges Suarez, *Briand, sa vie—son œuvre*, 6 vols., vol. VI, *L'Artisan de la paix 1923-1932* (Paris, 1952), pp. 222 ff.

given one volume of documents. Finally I was able to see to it
that we limited ourselves to the necessary questions. The military in general are ready to obey and accept commands. . . ."
Still, Briand continued, "there are a few remaining small points
to be settled. Why don't you see that they are taken care of?
Then I shall immediately give instructions to the French representative on the Conference of Ambassadors that the Military
Control Commission be withdrawn." Among these issues,
Briand added, there was one which caused him particular concern, and that was the patriotic associations. "The 'Stahlhelm,'"
he said, "issues a book of instructions with exact regulations about
military training, marksmanship, close order drill, etc. Naturally
my military show me these things and reproach me for viewing
Germany only with the eyes of the politician, not recognizing
what really is being prepared in Germany. Why doesn't the
German government suppress these things?"

Stresemann replied that he did not know the "Stahlhelm"
book, but the fact that it was sold publicly seemed to contra-
dict the secret nature of "Stahlhelm" training. He also denied
that the patriotic associations received Reichswehr support and
maintained that their main importance was psychological rather
than military. "The republic in Germany does not take into
account the psychological needs of the masses," he said. "It
stands rigidly in its dull, black frock coat. People want colour,
joy, movement, that is why the 'Stahlhelm' on the one hand
and the 'Reichsbanner' on the other have been so successful.
Minister of Defense Gessler once said that the soldier in the
past was successful with the girls because he gave them three
things: military music, uniforms, and love. The same is true
for the 'Stahlhelm' today."

Briand agreed with this idyllic picture of the patriotic associations as mere outlets for the German urge to play soldier. "Of
course it is always impressive," he continued Stresemann's argument, "to put on a steel helmet and act as though one were

still a great warrior. I don't attribute any decisive importance
to that either. But please see to it," he begged again, "that my
military can't always come to me with these things."

As far as the French Foreign Minister was concerned, the
foregoing is a further example of the impatience with which the
politician in him tried to ignore or, literally, "fling into a corner"
the arguments against the German army brought forth by his
military experts. The pettiness of these minor questions, he felt,
merely impeded the progress on larger issues.[31] It should cause
no surprise to find Stresemann agree to this generous attitude,
which was so favorable to Germany. The question is—did he
(or could he) share Briand's condescending attitude towards
the military, and could he honestly expect to "take care of the
few remaining points" on which Germany was still in default
in her disarmament? Was he not here "making his reckoning
without his host," as the German proverb goes, the host being
the Reichswehr? Briand himself seems to have felt some uneasiness on this point, because towards the end of the Thoiry
conversation he returned to it once again. "I have one urgent
plea," he told Stresemann, "and that is: watch your Reichswehr! I have a feeling that the Reichswehr is doing all manner
of things of which you have no knowledge. I don't consider
that too tragic. The military are the same everywhere. But our
policy must not suffer from it. I should feel a great deal easier
if incidents in this connection would stop."

Again Stresemann tried to dispel Briand's fears. "I admit,"
he said, "that by their very nature the military, whose task in
all states consists exclusively in preparing the defense of their
country, see things differently from statesmen. But I don't think
the things you mention are tragic. Herr von Seeckt is no illu-
sionist, but is fully aware of the situation in which Germany

[31] Suarez, *Briand*, VI, 222 ff. shows a somewhat less accommodating attitude on Briand's part.

finds herself. And the points raised by your side, after all, are matters of minor importance in which on our side only minor agencies are involved."

So much for the historic luncheon at Thoiry which, at the time, was thought to mark a turning point in Franco-German relations. As is generally known, the high hopes which both Briand, and especially Stresemann, had set upon the ultimate results of this meeting failed to materialize. It is impossible here to go into the many causes for this failure.[32] But among them was the inability or unwillingness on Stresemann's part to follow Briand's advice and try to subordinate the interests of the army to the declared aims of his foreign policy, with which these interests conflicted.[33] At first it appeared, though, as if a decisive change in the army High Command might facilitate the Foreign Minister's tasks. On October 8, three weeks after Thoiry, the world was startled by the sudden retirement of General von Seeckt from the leadership of the Reichswehr. Tempting as it may be, it would be wrong to see Seeckt's fall as a result of Thoiry or of Stresemann's efforts.[34] That there was an antagonism of long standing between the two we have already seen.

[32] For the most recent discussion, see Bretton, *Stresemann*, pp. 100 ff.

[33] H. R. Berndorf, in his book on Schleicher, *General zwischen Ost und West—Aus den Geheimnissen der Deutschen Republik* (Hamburg, 1951) p. 140, states: "With Stresemann, the era of the predominance of the politicians over the generals started in Germany." This somewhat dubious authority is cited by Henry Bernhard, "Seeckt und Stresemann," p. 473, in support of his own, slightly more qualified claim, that under Stresemann "the Reichswehr was subordinated to an almost genuine control of politics," and that Seeckt (as well as Schleicher) had to submit to "the political skill, the instinct, and finally the political energy of the leading brain of the times," i. e., Stresemann. Unintentionally, I am sure, Stresemann is here endowed with a degree of influence (and hence responsibility) over military as well as foreign affairs, which is not to that extent supported by the evidence thus far available.

[34] This, by implication at least, is done in Bretton, *Stresemann*, p. 102, and in Hubertus Prinz zu Löwenstein, *Stresemann. Das deutsche Schicksal im Spiegel seines Lebens* (Frankfurt a. M., 1952), pp. 297-298.

Nevertheless, in his heart-to-heart talk with Briand, Stresemann had repeatedly stressed Seeckt's moderation as far as German military preparedness was concerned; and there are a few indications even that personal relations between Seeckt and Stresemann had somewhat improved over the months just preceding.[35] At any rate, Stresemann himself denied afterwards that he had any hand in the dismissal of Seeckt.[36] And Seeckt, for his part, did not suspect any such participation, even though he was frank enough to say that he certainly was not justified "in expecting any personal sympathy from Herr Stresemann."[37] Stresemann, as Rabenau quite correctly puts it, was merely the beneficiary of a situation in the making of which he had no direct hand.[38] If Seeckt's relations with Stresemann had been strained, his relations with Gessler had not been much better. It is here that we find the direct cause for the general's retirement.[39] The presence, on Seeckt's authorization (and without Gessler's knowledge) of the ex-Crown Prince's eldest son at field exercises of the Reichswehr's crack Ninth Infantry Regiment may not in itself appear too earth-shaking an event. But it was only the latest in a long series of conflicts between the South German democrat Gessler and the Prussian Junker Seeckt, and this one came at a particularly critical time. Had Seeckt been able to count on Stresemann's support, he might have weathered the storm. But as things stood, his retirement could have nothing but favorable effects abroad. While it is correct, therefore, to say that Stresemann had no hand in Seeckt's dis-

---

[35] Stresemann, "Nachlass," 3145/7326/161390; Germany, Heeresarchiv Potsdam, "Papers of General Hans von Seeckt," Roll 11 (May 1926).

[36] Stresemann, "Nachlass," 3100/7137/149367 ff.

[37] Rabenau, Seeckt, pp. 552, 559.

[38] Ibid., p. 552.

[39] On Seeckt's dismissal see Reginald H. Phelps, "Aus den Seeckt-Dokumenten I," Deutsche Rundschau, LXXVIII, No. 9 (September 1952), pp. 881 ff. Phelps correctly calls Seeckt's fall "a transitory victory of the civil power in Germany over the military."

missal, it is equally true that their differing views on foreign
policy undoubtedly made Stresemann welcome such a move.
The army's loss, so it seemed, might easily be the Foreign
Minister's gain. If he had any serious intention of changing
his attitude towards the army's undercover violations of the
Versailles Treaty, here, certainly, was an opportunity. Seeckt's
successor, Major General Wilhelm Heye, was a type far different
from his predecessor. A competent officer, he neither had the
intellectual stature nor the ambition of Seeckt. At the same
time the benevolent, somewhat pompous "good uncle" Heye
was a great deal more approachable and easier to deal with than
the icy, silent "Sphinx" had been. As it turned out, neither
Heye nor any of his successors ever again wielded the influence
Seeckt had enjoyed before them—an influence, moreover, that
had by no means been completely eliminated.

But if one looks for any letup in Stresemann's efforts at
denying, explaining away, or screening German disarmament
violations, one looks in vain. For a fleeting moment it appeared
as though Germany were really willing to fulfill one of the
demands the Allies had made for some time: General Heye,
when appointed, was not the next in seniority to Seeckt, and
this fact was interpreted abroad as a sign that the German
government was at long last ready to subordinate the *Chef der
Heeresleitung* to the Reichswehrminister. The Conference of
Ambassadors, therefore, on October 20, decided that the question of the High Command had been settled satisfactorily. But
this decision proved premature, for on October 28, General
Heye was promoted to *General der Infanterie*, with seniority
as of December 1, 1924, thus becoming the senior ranking officer
on the Reichswehr's active list, just as Seeckt had been before
him.[40]

Yet there were other opportunities to show a change of heart,

[40] Toynbee, *Survey of International Affairs 1927*, p. 92; Taylor, *Sword
and Swastika*, p. 51.

if such a change had actually resulted from Seeckt's dismissal. Throughout October and November, Allied-German discussions continued to center around the remaining points on the list of German violations, in the hope of reaching agreement by the time the League Council convened in December, so that the transfer of supervision over German disarmament to the League of Nations might be settled at that time. On October 18, French *chargé d'affaires* Laboulaye again conveyed Briand's concern over the "Stahlhelm's" military activities.[41] But just as before and during the Thoiry meeting, Stresemann denied everything—or almost everything. In Saxony and Thuringia, where evidence of "Stahlhelm" training could not be denied, he admitted "exercises to counteract the communists, if such necessity should arise." The discussion continued on November 1, this time between Stresemann and French ambassador De Margerie. But first we should mention another meeting which took place on October 29, between Prussia's Minister President Braun, Gessler, and Stresemann. The Foreign Minister does not tell us what he himself said on that occasion, but he reports a long argument between the other two participants over illegal German rearmament measures to which he listened. Braun, among other things, told Gessler that he had heard about the construction of concrete dugouts near Küstrin, the labor being performed entirely by members of the "Stahlhelm"; and he added that other patriotic associations, such as the "Werwolf," were consulted about the political reliability of officer candidates. None of these things was denied by Gessler. He merely excused himself by stating that as long as Seeckt was in office there had been little he could do about this; but he promised that from now on everything would be different. Though he qualified this by adding: "In the East we must have somewhat more

[41] Stresemann, "Nachlass," 3147/7334/162755.

protection than we are entitled to under the Versailles Treaty,"
a statement that left the door open for further illegal activities.[42]

With this conversation still fresh in mind, Stresemann, three
days later, faced De Margerie to have what the *Vermächtnis*
rightly calls "an animated conversation."[43] De Margerie began
by raising the question of the Reichswehr High Command,
which had once again become acute with Heye's predated
promotion. Stresemann said he did not know much about it, but
claimed to see nothing peculiar in such a measure. The French
Ambassador then turned to a couple of other points which
Briand wanted cleared up. And then Stresemann on his own
launched into the problem which had come to overshadow all
others—the patriotic associations. He told De Margerie that he
had bought the "Stahlhelm" book Briand had told him about
at Thoiry, and had actually verified that it recommended to its
readers certain military manuals such as the one entitled: "How
do I train to become an infantryman?" But to infer from this
any military activity on the part of the "Stahlhelm," Stresemann said, was absurd, since it was impossible to train an army
simply by use of manuals. "In my opinion," he stated, "there
is hardly an organization in Germany aside from the [com-
munist] 'Roter Frontkämpferbund' that holds any regular military exercises. Certainly the two large organizations, the 'Stahlhelm' and the 'Jungdeutscher Orden' do not fall into this
category." And with an attempt at humour he added: "About
the 'Werwolf' I cannot give any opinion, since I have never
yet seen a werewolf. . . . Until I have exact proof, therefore,
that these associations actually engage in military exercises, I
cannot recommend to the cabinet any action against them."

Stresemann then went into the question of the relationship

---

[42] *Ibid.*, 3101/7155/151923-25; *ibid.*, 3147/7334/162851 ff.
[43] This account is based on Stresemann, "Nachlass," 3147/7334/162860 ff.,
which is considerably more complete, especially on military questions, than
the mutilated document in Stresemann, *Vermächtnis*, III, 45 ff.

between the Reichswehr and these associations. "I only recently asked Reichswehrminister Gessler," he told the French ambassador, "to urge General Heye to issue a declaration about the absence of any connection between the Reichswehr and these associations, similar to the one issued some time ago by the Reichswehrminister himself. The Reichswehrminister is absolutely opposed to such a connection and expects, as I think I know, to express this at a gathering of Reichswehr commanders." This certainly was not a very clear or positive statement. All it said was that Stresemann hoped Gessler, and maybe Heye, would disclaim any relationship between army and rightist organizations. How much weight such a disclaimer by persons so obviously prejudiced (and in the case of Gessler known for his lack of veracity) would carry, is a question De Margerie did not raise. But he told Stresemann that Germany's General von Pawelsz had "a mass of material" showing the military activities and relations of these associations. Whereupon the Foreign Minister said he was not familiar with this material and promised to examine it.

The French ambassador then mentioned the fortress of Königsberg and the Reichswehr's claims that all construction work there was simply necessary for purposes of maintenance. The Military Control Commission, De Margerie said, could not accept this explanation, and in Briand's opinion it would cause grave difficulties if the German government adopted a similar stand. Briand, the Ambassador concluded, could certainly not agree with recent German statements to the effect that "in the question of military control everything had been settled."

At this point, it seems, Stresemann's patience, sorely tried by the Ambassador's well-informed criticism, ran out. He denied having made anything like the above statement, and claimed he had merely said "that all essential points of disarmament had been settled, that the questions still pending were individual ones which could not affect disarmament in general, and that

German disarmament had been carried out." As for all the other objections De Margerie had raised, he brushed them aside as mere "naggings" (*Quengeleien*) and came back with a long series of his own, culminating in the guarded threat that there really seemed no sense in pursuing the policy of Thoiry any further, so it might be best to consider the whole negotiations finished.

De Margerie was deeply disturbed and showed it. He assured Stresemann that Briand and the whole French cabinet were very much interested in pursuing the Thoiry line further, and he begged him not to misunderstand what he had said earlier about military matters. All Briand was concerned over was the amicable collaboration between Germany and France at the December meeting of the League Council. It was for that reason that the few remaining military questions were to be cleared up. Stresemann replied that he, too, considered it *selbstverständlich* that military control had to be disposed of by December. "The German people," he added, "have a feeling that all these continued objections are raised merely in order to perpetuate the Military Control Commission for all eternity."

So much for the Stresemann–De Margerie conversation of November 1. There could now be little doubt in Stresemann's mind that the Allies were ready to withdraw their Military Control Commission if only sufficient German pressure were maintained. All through November negotiations continued, trying to remove the last obstacles in the way of such withdrawal. On November 9 and 18, Stresemann again told De Margerie that there was no question of any military activity on the part of the rightist associations, and in support he cited a declaration by the "Stahlhelm" itself, which specifically denied such activities.[44] "It is necessary," he told Britain's ambassador, "that the politicians set an end to the everlasting negotiations of the Inter-

---

[44] Stresemann, "Nachlass," 3147/7335/162979 ff., 163047 ff.

Allied Military Control Commission and the military experts." [45]
On November 23, the Foreign Minister, in a Reichstag address,
turned against "the further presence on German soil of foreign
control officers" as a "psychological burden" on the German
people. "German disarmament," he stated, "is complete, and
the few points on which negotiations with the other side are
still in progress, are no justification for the continued stay of
the Control Commission." Assuming that negotiations about disarmament were about to end, he thanked the "men of the
Reichswehr who participated in it" for the self-discipline they
had shown in carrying out their humiliating task that went
"against their best inner feelings." As for the patriotic associations, Stresemann pointed out that the German government had
taken steps to prevent their militarization, but that in any case
the whole matter was really one of domestic concern and hence
did not allow for the intervention of foreign powers. He also
promised that the government would strictly enforce its ruling
that no connection be established between these organizations
and the Reichswehr. [46]

After Stresemann had finished, the Reichswehrminister got
up to elaborate on this last point. And while Stresemann's statements had been greeted by applause from the parties of the
center, and with silence by those of the right and left, Gessler
was heckled in the most merciless fashion. "On every occasion,"
he began, "I have stated in the Reichstag my opposition towards
any relations between the Reichswehr and these military associations. (Laughter on the left.) I have prohibited most sharply
any connection of the Reichswehr with such associations and
have ruthlessly carried out this prohibition whenever violations
came to my attention. (Loud laughter and shouts on the left.)
Please wait a minute. (Delegate Höllein: Don't take us as being

[45] *Ibid.*, 3100/7137/149372.
[46] Germany, Reichstag, *Verhandlungen des Reichstags*, III. *Wahlperiode
1924*, vol. 391, pp. 8143-8144.

more stupid than we really are!—General laughter—Bell of the president). . . ." And so it went for the remainder of the minister's efforts at explaining his policy.[47] This uninhibited criticism of Gessler was not something new; it was merely an expression of a widely held distrust of his truthfulness. For almost seven years now he had been Minister of Defense, and during that time he had been called upon again and again to cover up the illegal activities of the Reichswehr. In the course of time he had developed a technique of using his South German joviality to divert attacks with a "mild hand," a technique which, though momentarily successful, never wholly convinced his adversaries. Stresemann's party-colleague Scholz once said that Gessler even excelled old admiral Tirpitz (who in his heyday had been labeled the "father of the lie") in the art of deception.[48] The Reichswehrminister on one occasion jokingly compared himself to a husband "who had no idea of his wife's infidelities, despite the fact that the whole town was talking about them."[49] How correctly this described his relations with the Reichswehr is difficult to say, though it is doubtful that he knew all the details of the army's clandestine operations, especially while Seeckt was in command. The fact that he had outlived his usefulness as a shield for such operations may have been one of the reasons that led to his retirement a year later.

In further pursuit of his determination to end Allied military control, Stresemann followed up his Reichstag declaration with a hint to Britain's new ambassador, Sir Ronald Lindsay, and to Briand's confidant, Professor Hesnard, that unless such control was abandoned, he might feel forced to resign.[50] The Allies at this time were debating a memorandum prepared by British military experts, which still listed the following "minimum program" which had to be fulfilled by Germany: subordination

[47] *Ibid.*, pp. 8145-8146.
[48] Stresemann, "Nachlass," 3167/7338/163583.
[49] Severing, *Mein Lebensweg*, II, 117.
[50] Stresemann, "Nachlass," 3167/7336/163175 ff., 163182.

of the commander-in-chief of the Reichswehr to the authority
of the Reichswehrminister; settlement of the question of recruiting and of patriotic associations; control of the export of
arms and munitions; and destruction of the new fortifications
on Germany's eastern frontier.[51] By the beginning of December,
these points had been whittled down to two: export of war
materials and eastern fortifications. Even so, the French still
expressed uneasiness over the military activities of the patriotic
associations and their relations with the Reichswehr.[52]

Before turning to the hurried and unceremonious burial of
Allied Military Control at the turn of the year, we must take
another brief look behind the scenes to see how Stresemann's
protestations of complete German disarmament stacked up
against the facts. On December 1, a meeting took place at the
Foreign Office between representatives of the government (Chancellor Marx, Gessler, and Stresemann) and a number of prominent Social Democrats (Müller, Wels, Breitscheid, Scheidemann,
and Eggerstedt).[53] Its purpose was to discuss a long list of
Reichswehr disarmament violations which Scheidemann had
drawn up and which he now presented with a mixture of indignation and concern. "If these things became known," the
socialist deputy said, "the policy of Stresemann would explode."
Most of Scheidemann's material dealt with Russo-German military relations, which we shall discuss at greater length below.
But there was also information on the recruiting of Reichswehr
members from nationalist organizations, on the camouflaging
of such organizations as athletic clubs, on their relations with the
German navy,[54] on the production of poison gas in Germany,
etc. Gessler did not deny any of the points raised, though he
claimed to be hearing about some of them for the first time.

[51] *Schulthess*, vol. 67 (1926), pp. 447-448.
[52] Toynbee, *Survey of International Affairs 1927*, p. 94.
[53] Robert M. W. Kempner, "Die Reichswehr und die Reichsregierung,"
Der Monat, I, No. 6 (March 1949), pp. 103-105.
[54] The efforts of the German navy to evade the restrictions of Versailles

On others he himself elaborated, telling, for instance, that Germany had built some 300 airplanes per year in Russian factories, of which Russia received 100, leaving 200 for Germany. The production of ammunition in the Soviet Union he defended as necessary in view of Allied prohibition against such production in Germany. But all this, the Reichswehrminister assured the socialists, was to be different, now that Seeckt had gone. He had discussed all Reichswehr matters with Heye and with the cabinet, and he felt certain that he would be able to bring about some changes—except on the eastern borders, where Germany would continue to need protection. Stresemann spoke only once, according to our report. He asked Gessler whether any more deliveries of Russian ammunition were expected, and Gessler said "no." This seemed to satisfy the Foreign Minister. Scheidemann, on the other hand, was put off less easily. He referred rather pointedly to the unreliability of Gessler's past statements on disarmament, and he elicited a promise from the Reichswehrminister that his allegations would be carefully examined and a new meeting called to discuss the matter further.

Less than a week later, on December 6, the League Council was scheduled to meet, and high up on its agenda was the shift of military control from the Allied Conference of Ambassadors and its Control Commission to the League of Nations. The question that had occupied both Germans and Allies for some time was how the League's supervisory powers should be carried out.[55] As early as the fall of 1924, the League had

did not cause as much trouble with the Allies as those of the army and hence did not attract much attention from Stresemann. Naval violations, while smaller in scope and without the guiding hand of a man like Seeckt, still had most of the characteristics we found in similar activities of the army: secret arsenals, training of short-term volunteers, use of forbidden weapons, etc. See "The Fight of the Navy against Versailles, 1919-1935," published in 1937 by the High Command of the German Navy, in: Germany, U. S. Zone of Occupation, Military Tribunals, *Trials of War Criminals*, X, 433 ff.

[55] For this and the following see Toynbee, *Survey of International Affairs 1927*, pp. 85-86, 94-95.

adopted a scheme for setting up Commissions of Investigation to deal with cases where League action seemed indicated. But it was known that the German government had several objections to this scheme, notably to its provision for the establishment of a permanent or semipermanent organ of investigation in the demilitarized zone of the Rhineland. Stresemann had made it quite clear from the start that the League should not simply continue the functions of the Allied Control Commission.[56] He had also mentioned the matter at Thoiry, and at that time Briand had assured him that the whole thing was pretty theoretical, and that "nobody really thought of carrying out any investigation of a League member." "I shall concur as a matter of course," he had added, "with everything the legal experts will decide in agreement with you. We only need find some kind of formula which will maintain the right of the League to carry out a certain control."[57] Negotiations over this problem were still in progress during the opening days of the League Council meeting, but finally, on December 9, Germany's objections were met and agreement was reached. Any special form of investigation for the demilitarized part of western Germany, or any other permanent control would henceforth require the consent of Germany.[58]

With this question cleared up, there now remained only the few disputed points of German disarmament on which Allied and German experts could not agree. On December 10, the Conference of Ambassadors reported that Germany still had not met Allied objections on the export of war materials and on eastern fortifications. But this no longer made much impression on the foreign ministers assembled at Geneva. The following day, December 11, they decided that the Inter-Allied Control Commission should be withdrawn from Germany by January

---

[56] See above, p. 20.

[57] Stresemann, *Vermächtnis*, III, 23.

[58] For the deliberations of the League Council see Toynbee, *Survey of International Affairs 1927*, pp. 97-98; *Schulthess*, vol. 67 (1926), pp. 495-498.

31, 1927. If the disarmament questions still pending had not been settled by then, they should be referred to the League Council. For the next six weeks negotiations over the remaining two points continued. But when the end of January finally came around, the Conference of Ambassadors was still not satisfied with Germany's fulfillment of these points. Stresemann, a few days earlier, had told representatives of the German Nationalist People's Party that negotiations were being dragged out on purpose by Germany, so that she could get away with making fewer concessions.[59]

All this, however, did not affect the main issue. The Allied Military Control Commission was withdrawn, as scheduled, on January 31, 1927. Again the Allies had lived up to their side of an agreement, as they had done exactly a year earlier, without waiting for Germany to do her share. Prior to its withdrawal, the Control Commission had issued a final report, a lengthy document of some 500 pages, which stated that "Germany had never disarmed, had never had the intention of disarming, and for seven years had done everything in her power to deceive and 'counter-control' the Commission appointed to control her disarmament." But the report was "deliberately ignored and suppressed."[60] As Professor Toynbee wrote, approvingly, a year or so later: "It was no longer possible that a settlement should be delayed indefinitely by technical controversies between experts now that the statesmen were of one mind in feeling that the time for a settlement had come and were also in agreement over the broad lines of their political bargain."[61] On December 9, the three main partners in this political bargain—Briand, Chamberlain, and Stresemann—were awarded the Nobel Peace Prize. The "Spirit of Locarno" was in full flower.

[59] Stresemann, "Nachlass," 3167/7338/163628.
[60] Wheeler-Bennett, The Nemesis of Power, pp. 185-186; see also Morgan, Assize of Arms, Introduction.
[61] Toynbee, Survey of International Affairs 1927, p. 96.

IV The Reichswehr and Russia

THE VICTORY WHICH Stresemann had just won, the withdrawal of Allied military control, was a greater one than he had achieved a year before. At that time the issue had been Allied withdrawal from the northern Rhineland, a move provided for in the Versailles settlement. This time he had gone beyond and had "successfully revised the substance, if not the letter, of the disarmament clauses of the Treaty of Versailles." [1] The formal restrictions of the Treaty remained, of course, but the means of enforcing them now had been abandoned. Most of the credit for this belongs to him, to the singleness of purpose and the infinite patience with which he gradually extricated his country from the restrictions of a treaty from which there was no other escape. But as was pointed out above, Stresemann's task had been materially aided by a gradual relaxation of Allied watchfulness towards Germany. How far this had gone was shown in the crucial weeks of December 1926, when the withdrawal of military control was decided by Allied politicians not only against the advice of their own military experts, but in the face of disturbing reports from inside Germany as well.

The meeting of December 1 between leading members of the German cabinet and its socialist critics, at which Scheidemann had claimed that Germany was far from disarmed, had set in

[1] Bretton, *Stresemann*, pp. 144-145.

motion a series of events which might easily at the last minute have defeated Stresemann's efforts at liberating his country from military control.[2] On December 2, the *Manchester Guardian* carried an article on Russo-German military collaboration which repeated some of Scheidemann's revelations on the previous day. From there the information seeped into the socialist *Vorwärts*, causing a state of high alarm in the German Foreign Office because of the danger such disclosures presented to Stresemann's foreign policy.[3] But the real shock was yet to come. When Gessler's promise of December 1 that he would examine Scheidemann's criticism of the Reichswehr did not bring any satisfactory results, the socialists decided to go one step further and bring the matter out into the open.[4] This was done in a sensational speech which Scheidemann, at the instigation of his party, delivered before the Reichstag on December 16. Whether the socialists in taking this radical step were motivated primarily by concern over the Reichswehr's secret activities, or whether their real aim was to bring about a crisis and subsequent reorganization of the government, is immaterial here.[5] The important point is that never before in Germany had such detailed disclosures been made in public, disclosures, moreover, which since then have been proved substantially correct.

Scheidemann started out by accusing the Reichswehr of having developed into "a state within the state, following its own laws and carrying on its own policy." To support his charge, the socialist deputy dealt with three major points: the financing of illegal rearmament, the relations between the army and radical

[2] See above, pp. 68-69.

[3] Gustav Hilger and Alfred G. Meyer, *The Incompatible Allies—A Memoir-History of German-Soviet Relations 1918-1941* (New York, 1953), pp. 188, 203-204.

[4] Friedrich Stampfer, *Die ersten vierzehn Jahre der Deutschen Republik* (2d ed., Offenbach, 1947), pp. 493-494.

[5] Severing, *Mein Lebensweg*, II, 103-104; Stresemann, *Vermächtnis*, III, 90-93.

rightist organizations, and the Reichswehr's dealings with Soviet Russia.[6] On the first he was rather brief, but he still cited sufficient evidence to illustrate his contention that vast funds were spent every year for purposes that could not be openly revealed in the army budget, and that a large share of these funds came from private sources. Even these relatively mild revelations caused infuriated shouts of "traitor!", "throw him out!" from the parties of the right, and before he had finished with the first point the *Deutschnationalen* and the *Völkischen* (which included the few Nazi delegates) had left by way of protest. It was only due to Stresemann's intervention that his own party did not join in the exodus.[7] With most of the opposition out of the way, Scheidemann then launched into the second part of his speech, in which, with staggering detail, he told of the many different ways in which the army was trying to increase its reserves of manpower by maintaining close contacts with those semimilitary patriotic associations which had so aroused French fears. The real revelations, however, came with the last section of his address, when the socialist deputy repeated and elaborated upon the relations between the Reichswehr and Russia, notably upon the production of airplanes, poison gas, and ammunition by German firms in the Soviet Union. Among other things Scheidemann told of the arrival of Russian grenades at the German port of Stettin as recently as early October. During this part of the speech the interruptions which earlier had come from the right, now came from the communists, to whom these disclosures of Russian assistance to German rearmament, naturally, were most embarrassing.[8] Scheidemann did point out, however, that in his opinion German

[6] Germany, Reichstag, *Verhandlungen*, vol. 391, pp. 8577-8586.

[7] Stresemann, "Nachlass," 3167/7337/163465.

[8] See Hans Rothfels in Helm Speidel, "Reichswehr und Rote Armee," p. 11. As Rothfels points out, this part of Scheidemann's speech was more directed against Russia and against the German communists than against the Reichswehr.

secret rearmament was vastly overrated abroad and that Germany
was far too weak to wage a successful war. "But if we ignore
all these things," he added, "and thus give the impression as
though, by silence, we condone them, the foreign policy conducted at present by Herr Stresemann becomes impossible. We
must make it clear that the majority of the German people will
have no part of these things, and that we want to keep honestly
the treaties Germany has concluded."

When Scheidemann had finished, Chancellor Marx rose to
reply.[9] He felt only the "deepest regret," he said that the deputy
had spoken the way he did. As to the specific incidents cited,
Marx claimed they either happened long ago or under quite
different circumstances and hence should not be brought up at
this time. Scheidemann's one-sided presentation, he added, gave
a wholly false picture of conditions in the Reichswehr, and he
thanked the latter for its "quiet and selfless work in the service
of the fatherland."

The general tenor and evasiveness of the Chancellor's reply
certainly seemed to indicate that Scheidemann's revelations had
come pretty close to the truth. But if any repercussions abroad
had been feared, such fears proved unfounded. Scheidemann
himself had pointed out at the beginning that what he had to
say was already general knowledge outside Germany. As the
Baltimore Sun quite confidently put it: "All of the information
that Scheidemann has blurted out in the Reichstag has, beyond
doubt, been in the hands of the statesmen of the Allied
nations."[10] Scheidemann, after all, was merely repeating what
Allied military experts had been saying for the past seven years—
with one exception, that is: in our discussion thus far there has
been no evidence that the Allies had any inkling of the Reichswehr's military relations with the Soviet Union. But while this
opened up a whole new perspective on German rearmament,

[9] Germany, Reichstag, *Verhandlungen*, vol. 391, pp. 8586-8587.
[10] Quoted in Taylor, *Sword and Swastika*, p. 50.

strictly speaking it had nothing to do with the immediate issue, the withdrawal of Allied military control. The Soviet Union was neither a signatory to the Treaty of Versailles nor a member of the League of Nations, and hence was perfectly free to maintain whatever relations she chose with the German army. And as far as Germany was concerned, any effective control by Allied officers over such relations was impossible as long as they took place on Russian soil. If one of the main efforts of Allied policy during the Locarno era was to wean the Reich away from Russia, the maintenance of Allied military control would only have been detrimental to such a course since it might have served to strengthen the ties between Reichswehr and Red Army and thus make Germany more dependent on the Soviet Union.[11] The Allies faced the alternative of either returning to the strict enforcement of each and every provision of Versailles, which would have meant the end of Locarno and all it had come to signify; or else they had to close their eyes to many things that went on in Germany, putting their trust in the good will of Stresemann, who would see to it that his country lived up to obligations voluntarily undertaken. By the end of 1927, the western powers had gone too far along the second path to turn back.

What was Stresemann's reaction to Scheidemann's speech? The evening of the day on which it was delivered, the Foreign Minister himself addressed a closed meeting of local dignitaries in faraway Königsberg on the role of eastern problems in his outwardly westerly policy.[12] "Our western policy," he said,

---

[11] Hallgarten, "General Hans von Seeckt and Russia," p. 29. Hallgarten somewhat overstresses the significance of the Locarno policy as a turning point bringing about the "transfer [of] the main theater of rearmament from Russia to German soil." There was a good deal of illegal rearmament in Germany prior to Locarno and activities in Russia, as we shall see, continued long after Locarno.

[12] This is based on the account in Stresemann, "Nachlass," 3173/7372/

"rests upon and proceeds from our eastern policy." Yet he cautioned his audience against expecting any direct military aid from the Soviet Union. "In 1813 Prussia put everything on the one Russian card," Stresemann explained; "but Versailles is worse than Tilsit. The present equivalent of the 42,000 man army which Prussia was permitted at that time would be 400,000. Furthermore, Russian armies in general have no offensive force. A Russian army that entered the Reich as an ally would at best try to Bolshevize Germany." The only alternative for Germany, he concluded, was "to file off the fetters" of Versailles.

There was no reference here to any of Scheidemann's revelations, which hardly came as a surprise to the Foreign Minister. A day or two before the crucial Reichstag session, a group of socialists, including Scheidemann, had called upon Marx, Gessler, and Stresemann to continue the inconclusive discussion of December 1, and especially to find out more about Russia's deliveries of grenades to the Reichswehr.[18] Gessler explained that the latter were "the result of German foreign policy and the logical continuation of the Rapallo policy initiated by Chancellor Wirth." "Nothing has been done," he added, "of which the Foreign Office did not have knowledge. The necessary false passports were issued in the Foreign Office." This was Stresemann's department, and he immediately called his Secretary of State, von Schubert, to check on the passport matter. He was told that Gessler's statement was incorrect. As far as any other participation of his ministry was concerned, Stresemann admitted that upon becoming Chancellor in 1923, his predecessor Cuno had told him that "thirty million marks were due [presumably to Russia] on the basis of earlier agreements." This amount, Stresemann said, he authorized to be paid, after President Ebert

166866 ff., rather than on the abbreviated version in Stresemann, *Vermächtnis*, III, 247-249.
[18] Stresemann, "Nachlass," 3167/7337/163462. These excerpts from Stresemann's diary have been omitted in Stresemann, *Vermächtnis*, III, 91.

gave his approval. But at the same time he agreed with Ebert that Russo-German military relations "must be considered broken off once and for all"; and more recently, Stresemann concluded, the Foreign Office had not been involved in any such relations. So much for Stresemann's modifications of Gessler's claims. There is no record of any reply by the Reichswehr-minister, but he promised again to examine the material presented by the socialists and to give a later reply.

When this reply was not forthcoming, the socialist delegation, on the eve of Scheidemann's speech, again approached the government and again received no satisfactory reply.[14] At this point they must have declared their determination to bring the matter before the Reichstag. "We are arranging with the socialists," Stresemann wrote in his diary, "to have them request explanations about the Reichswehr only on specific points, and I shall brief them how Marx will reply to these points. In answer to a question from me, Hermann Müller says that there was of course no intention of touching on the Russian question and on the question of 'border guards.'" In other words, the details of the next day's showdown had been prearranged. But the socialists, as we have seen, did not live up to this prearrangement, especially in regard to Russia, a fact which caused embarrassment to the government and necessitated a last minute revision of the Chancellor's reply. Marx actually suggested that the cabinet leave the Reichstag in protest, but Stresemann advised against it, since such a move would only add weight to Scheidemann's statements. Instead, he tells us, he drew up "a few sentences for the declaration which Marx delivered on the accusations made against the Reichswehr." The verbal exchange on December 16, in other words, was essentially one between Scheidemann and Stresemann.

Before going into the effect which Scheidemann's disclosures

---

[14] Stresemann, "Nachlass," 3167/7337/163463-65.

had upon future relations between the Reichswehr and Russia, we must try to throw some light on the role, if any, which Stresemann and the Foreign Office had up to this point played in these relations. The Foreign Minister, as was just shown, admitted that he knew as far back as 1923 that some sort of secret military ties existed between his country and the Soviet Union; but he also claimed that he had insisted that these ties be broken off and that his office had not recently been involved in these matters. The Reichswehr's dealings with Russia, because of the deep secrecy in which they were kept, are still one of the lesser-known chapters in the history of the Weimar Republic.[15] References to it in Stresemann's papers are very few, but from available evidence it is clear that the Foreign Minister was never a hindrance and at times was quite a help to Russo-German military collaboration. Of all the army's clandestine operations, this one, of course, was potentially the most dangerous, since it might easily discredit Stresemann's policy in western eyes. On the other hand, the danger it presented in the West was partly compensated by advantages in the East. In Germany's relations with Russia, the Reichswehr's collaboration with the Red Army had a certain stabilizing effect, which aided the maintenance of political and economic friendship between the two countries despite Germany's rapprochement with the West at Locarno.[16] And such friendly relations with Russia in turn proved a valuable asset in Stresemann's negotiations with the West.

[15] For the most authoritative account to date of Russo-German military collaboration, see Speidel, " Reichswehr und Rote Armee," with an excellent introduction by Hans Rothfels; see also Carr, *German-Soviet Relations*, chs. III-V; Hilger and Meyer, *The Incompatible Allies*, pp. 189 ff.

[16] Speidel, " Reichswehr und Rote Armee," p. 15. Stresemann's policy towards Russia bears further investigation which may show that he did not differ as markedly from his Moscow ambassador, Count Brockdorff-Rantzau, as has been assumed by some writers, *e. g.*, Felix Hirsch, " Stresemann in Historical Perspective," p. 374.

Of course it would be wrong to assume that Stresemann knew all the details of Russo-German military relations. These were known only to a small clique within the Reichswehr, at the head of which, until his retirement, was General von Seeckt, who more than anyone else was the architect of the army's Russian policy. Secrecy about these matters, according to one of the participants, even within the Reichswehrministry itself, "was almost elevated into a cult," and only those officers whose assistance was essential were initiated into the Russian secret.[17] It seems that in the initial stages, the German Foreign Ministry had played its part in establishing military contacts with Russia. The contract between the Soviet government and the German firm of Junkers, for instance, which enabled the latter to produce airplanes in Russia had been concluded with the aid of the Foreign Office.[18] But as time went on, the Reichswehr's military missions became more and more independent, much to the chagrin of ambassador Brockdorff-Rantzau, who was worried lest Russia gain an advantage over Germany in these dealings and who hoped to make political capital for Germany out of her relations with the Red Army. It was only after considerable effort on the ambassador's part that by 1923 he "succeeded at least in compelling the cabinet to assume a certain amount of control over the matter of military collaboration." As a result, the German Embassy in Moscow from then on was officially "in control of military agreements";[19] and in the absence of a military attaché, it was the ambassador himself who took a hand in these affairs.

This is borne out by a lengthy and secret report on a conversation between himself and Trotsky, which Brockdorff sent to

[17] Speidel, "Reichswehr und Rote Armee," pp. 31-32.
[18] Hilger and Meyer, *The Incompatible Allies*, pp. 199-200. Hilger for many years was a member of the German embassy in Moscow, which makes his account particularly valuable.
[19] *Ibid.*, p. 201.

Stresemann in June 1924.[20] The ambassador reproached the People's Commissar for various major and minor obstacles that had beset German rearmament efforts in Russia during the preceding months: certain German officers had been received rather coolly by Soviet officials, a Junkers plane scheduled to participate in the May Day Parade had been barred, the Junkers works in Russia had not received sufficient Russian orders, the rifle-works at Tula, which were under German management, had been inspected by a visiting commission of English or American officers, a German mission which hoped to negotiate for ten of Germany's best flyers to be admitted to Russia was not making sufficient headway, etc. The very detail of the points shows the familiarity Brockdorff-Rantzau had with Russo-German military relations and the role he played in seeing to it that these activities proceeded as smoothly as possible.[21] Stresemann forwarded copies of the report with a noncommittal note to Gessler and Seeckt.[22]

Due to the small number of persons involved in these dealings with Russia, hardly any news of them ever leaked out. There had been rumours since the Treaty of Rapallo in 1922, that it contained a secret military appendix, but they were never substantiated. Shortly after taking office, in November 1923, Stresemann denied categorically to his friend D'Abernon that Germany maintained any armament factories in Russia.[23] But the matter seems to have preyed on the Ambassador's mind. "I still hold," he wrote in 1925, "that prolonged co-operation between the German Right and the Russian Left is unthinkable, but I must admit that the other night at the Russian Embassy

[20] Stresemann, "Nachlass," 3165/7414/175334 ff.

[21] This material disproves the statement in Eugen Fischer-Baling, "Politik und Kriegsromantik," Der Monat, I, No. 2 (November 1948), p. 55, that Brockdorff-Rantzau had no hand in Russo-German military dealings.

[22] Stresemann, "Nachlass," 3165/7414/175333.

[23] D'Abernon, Diary, II, 289.

I was somewhat shaken to see how many gentlemen there were with stiff military backs and breasts bedecked with iron crosses, all partaking freely of Soviet champagne." [24] Late in 1925, when Seeckt entertained Foreign Commissar Chicherin at lunch, the German press began to speculate on possible Russo-German military ventures. But the Foreign Ministry immediately stepped in to dispel such rumours. "Upon the suggestion of the Wilhelmstrasse, the *Kreuz Zeitung* declared the meeting to have been a courtesy visit, purely a matter of form, at which, moreover, two officials from the Foreign Office had been present to prevent any unauthorized deals." [25]

In early 1926, Russia's Vice Commissar of War, Unshlikht, hiding behind the name of "Herr Untermann," visited Berlin and made a series of far-reaching proposals to Stresemann, Seeckt, and other members of the cabinet concerning the construction of plants in Russia "for the manufacturing of heavy artillery, chemical-warfare stuffs, precision instruments, and other material which the Versailles Treaty prohibited Germany from owning or using. He proposed that officer-training schools be connected with these industrial enterprises." Gustav Hilger, who tells of this Russian visit, states that he does not know whether Unshlikht's proposals ever materialized in full, but adds that "German technical and medical experts were still in the Soviet Union at the end of 1926 to assist in experiments with new chemicals." [26] Around this same time, Stresemann's secretary, in a memorandum for the Foreign Minister's information, spoke of "the innumerable connections between the Reichswehr and Soviet Russia which, the Reichswehr claims, are carried on in agreement with the Foreign Office." [27] Again a few

[24] *Ibid.*, III, 205.
[25] Hilger and Meyer, *The Incompatible Allies*, pp. 187-188; see also *ibid.*, p. 189, n. 1, on further rumours in the press about German-Soviet military relations.
[26] *Ibid.*, p. 202.
[27] Stresemann, "Nachlass," 3100/7138/149467.

months later, in August 1926, there is a note by Stresemann himself on a report from Brockdorff-Rantzau that 400,000 Russian grenades were ready for delivery to Germany. The Ambassador had warned the army that "if this matter became known, it would compromise [Germany's] foreign policy"; but the Reichswehr had assured him that great care would be taken so that nothing leaked out. Of a simultaneous report that German ships, carrying poison gas to Russia, had made an emergency landing in Finland, the Reichswehr Ministry disclaimed any knowledge.[28]

There is a further note by Stresemann, the date of which is not quite certain, but it must have been written after Seeckt's retirement, probably late in 1926.[29] "Ambassador Brockdorff-Rantzau," it says, "told me during his visit that the Reichswehr intends to continue Russo-German military relations. The question under discussion concerns payment for a factory to produce tanks and another factory for [poison] gas." Russia, the Ambassador added, had raised some difficulties about these plans because she did not quite trust Defense Minister Gessler's discretion in these matters. "The Reichswehrminister," Stresemann's note continues, "will probably approach me on this. I shall present the case quite frankly to General Heye."

Except for this last sentence, there is no indication of Stresemann's taking any action on the reports he received from various quarters about the secret dealings between the Reichswehr and Russia. And here we cannot be quite certain what stand he took when talking to Heye. But even if we assume, for lack of more definite proof, that Stresemann, during the critical years when he was trying to rid Germany of Allied military control, did not actively further this Russo-German collaboration, his Foreign Office and foreign service certainly did. According to General Helm Speidel, who during the twenties and early thirties partici-

[28] *Ibid.*, 3100/7137/149293.
[29] *Ibid.*, 3112/7128/147736.

pated in these operations, the political problems connected with such collaboration "were settled in co-operation with the Foreign Office." The German officers on their way to and from Russia used false names but "genuine passports with valid visas," and their official as well as private mail was sent through "the courier service of the German Embassy or the Foreign Office." To illustrate this co-operation between Reichswehr and foreign service, Speidel presents a diagram showing the interrelationship of the various German agencies concerned with Russo-German military relations, and here "collaboration" (*Zusammenarbeit*) is indicated between the *Truppenamt* (General Staff) and the Foreign Office in Berlin, as well as between the Reichswehr's *Zentrale Moskau* and the German Embassy in Moscow. The *Zentrale Moskau*, or 'Z. Mo.' as it was called, "worked with the German Embassy, whose aid in political questions it used. 'Z. Mo.' did not engage in politics on its own but was the organ on the one hand, of the Reichswehrministry in Berlin and on the other of the German Embassy in Moscow." [30] Gustav Hilger's reports on his activities as member of the Moscow Embassy and on his inspection trips to Soviet armament factories bear out Speidel's account, as do the activities of Brockdorff-Rantzau mentioned above. [31] To be sure, the evidence we have does not conclusively prove Stresemann's participation in this *Zusammenarbeit*. But it is difficult to conceive that these important arrangements existed without the knowledge and consent of the Foreign Minister. [32] If he avoided any too overt involvement in these matters, this was probably due to his fear that they might endanger his policy in the West. [33] Yet

[30] Speidel, "Reichswehr und Rote Armee," pp. 19-20, 33-34, 43.

[31] Hilger and Meyer, *The Incompatible Allies*, p. 195.

[32] This writer does not accept the conclusion in Bretton, *Stresemann*, p. 144, that "Stresemann succeeded in remaining aloof from the entire conspiracy" between Reichswehr and Red Army, since "he was well aware of the Soviet government's long-range plans and aspirations."

[33] The fact that Russo-German military relations were primarily the province

there is no indication that such fear ever moved him to use his influence to break up the Russo-German conspiracy.

If there ever was an opportunity to sever these Russian ties, it was in connection with Scheidemann's embarrassing disclosures in December 1926, following so shortly upon the retirement of Seeckt, who had been the chief German supporter of these ties. But this idea never seems to have entered anyone's mind. We have already seen how Stresemann, before the socialist deputy's speech, had tried to keep him from making any references to Russia, and how during the speech itself he had taken a hand in trying to minimize its effect. But despite such efforts, its impact was felt widely, both in army and civilian circles. "In the Foreign Ministry and in the Embassy in Moscow," Hilger tells us, "the mood was one of sadness and anger over the fact that the socialists could let considerations of partisan politics override what many of my colleagues thought was the national interest." [34] Major Fritz Tschunke, one of the main agents on the German side in the army's Russian policy, calls Scheidemann's speech "a heavy blow" to his work.[35] The Russians, outwardly at least, reacted more calmly. Chicherin, in an interview in the *Berliner Tageblatt* brushed aside Scheidemann's disclosures as "Made in England"; and both *Pravda* and *Izvestiya*, while admitting the establishment of war industries by German firms in Russia, remained silent on the export of war material to Germany and the training of German personnel in the Soviet Union.[36] But underneath the Russians were deeply disturbed. Soviet ambassador Krestinski called on Stresemann in early January and expressed his government's alarm over the revelations made by Scheidemann and the

of his adversary von Seeckt likewise may have influenced Stresemann's attitude prior to Seeckt's retirement.

[34] Hilger and Meyer, *The Incompatible Allies*, p. 203.

[35] Julius Epstein, "Der Seeckt Plan," *Der Monat*, I, No. 2 (November 1948), p. 49.

[36] Carr, *German-Soviet Relations*, p. 94.

Manchester Guardian. He suggested that the German government would do best to deny everything; but Stresemann said that that was impossible, since the Finnish government had already informed France and Great Britain of the emergency landing of German ships carrying war materials between Leningrad and Stettin. He promised, however, to consult with the Russians before any statement on the matter was issued.[37]

The major worry of the German Foreign Office at this time seems to have been not so much how to explain Scheidemann's exposures to the western powers—as we saw they pretty well ignored the whole affair—but how to quiet the suspicions which these exposures had aroused among the German socialists. The matter was bound to come before the Reichstag's Foreign Affairs Committee, and both Reichswehr and Foreign Office tried to have the Committee's next meeting cancelled, so as to avoid the inevitable showdown.[38] When this proved impossible, von Dirksen of the Foreign Office and Colonel Fischer of the army prepared a joint statement, which they showed to the Russian Embassy before the meeting. And since it revealed nothing that either Scheidemann or the newspapers had not told already, the Russians were satisfied. The meeting of the Committee took place in early February. And thanks to careful teamwork between the Foreign Office and Gessler, who discussed matters beforehand with the socialists, the expected storm was averted. Some of the socialists already had criticized Scheidemann for his rash utterances.[39] At the meeting itself, socialist ex-Chancellor Hermann Müller admitted that "he, too, had helped rock the Russian cradle"; and former Chancellor Wirth again told of his own share in German illegal rearmament during the early twenties, as he had already done in the Reichstag

[37] Stresemann, "Nachlass," 3167/7337/163495-96.
[38] On this and the following, unless otherwise indicated, see Hilger and Meyer, *The Incompatible Allies,* pp. 204-205.
[39] Stampfer, *Deutsche Republik,* p. 494.

meeting on December 16.[40] As a result everything went very smoothly. Secretary of State von Schubert, who in the absence of Stresemann conducted the meeting, stressed the necessity for careful German maneuvering between the East and West which would leave Germany freedom of action in every direction, and the parties present agreed. "Herr von Schubert," one of the participants told Stresemann, "was radiant" with pleasure over the outcome of the meeting, as well he might have been.[41]

Henceforward we know even less of what went on between the Reichswehr and the Red Army than we do for the earlier period. Considering the events of December, greater security precautions were taken now than ever before. When Seeckt planned to visit Russia in early 1927, he was dissuaded by the Foreign Office for fear that his trip would arouse renewed suspicion.[42] Actually it seems that the Russians were more worried than the Germans, according to a letter from Colonel Fischer to Seeckt in March 1927, which also stated that the German Foreign Office had "declared its agreement with the way in which our work is being carried on." One thing is certain: the Reichswehr's collaboration with Russia was not interrupted or even seriously disturbed by Scheidemann's revelations—if anything, it was intensified. Stresemann, according to Hilger, "gave his approval to the continued operation of the schools at Lipetsk and Kazan."[43] More German officers passed through the *Zentrale Moskau* than ever before, and more high-ranking German military figures now visited the Soviet Union (traveling in mufti

[40] Germany, Reichstag, *Verhandlungen*, vol. 391, pp. 8588-8595.
[41] Stresemann, "Nachlass," 3148/7340/163920.
[42] Hilger and Meyer, *The Incompatible Allies*, p. 206.
[43] *Ibid.*, p. 205. Lipetsk was a training center for the illegal German air force (founded in 1924) and Kazan a training-school for tank warfare (founded, according to Speidel, "about 1930"). The only other center besides Lipetsk that existed in Stresemann's time was the training-school for gas warfare known by the code-name "Tomka" (founded about 1927/28). See Speidel, "Reichswehr und Rote Armee," pp. 18, 26, 36.

as "Communist German Workers' Delegations") to participate
in maneuvers of the Red Army. The German government may
have feared that German termination of its Russian contacts
would make the Russians turn elsewhere, to France perhaps,
for the aid which Germany was giving them in building up
their armament industry. And besides, even if Germany's political leaders should decide to discontinue their participation in
the military dealings with Russia, there was no guarantee that
the Reichswehr would follow their lead. "Thus the Foreign
Office," Hilger concludes, "capitulated to the generals with the
greatest of pleasure. All concerned, from Stresemann on down,
were resolved not only to continue as before with military
co-operation, but to intensify it, though with the greatest
caution." [44]

---

[44] Hilger and Meyer, *The Incompatible Allies*, pp. 205, 207.

V | The perfection of German rearmament

WITH FOREIGN MILITARY control safely dispatched and the domestic criticism raised by Scheidemann's speech effectively quieted, the Reichswehr at the beginning of 1927 felt it could finally settle down to some undisturbed rearming. Of the two potential dangers to such illegal activity, the more serious one from now on threatened to come from inside rather than outside Germany. Once the few issues still pending between Germany and the Allies had been settled, the debate outside turned almost entirely to the question of general disarmament or, if that seemed unfeasible, to Germany's right to equal armament. As Stresemann had stated the problem to a Hamburg audience back in December 1926: German disarmament, he said, was "an important step, but only a step. For I must frankly say that it is an impossible situation, incompatible with equality under the League of Nations, to maintain universal preparedness while at the same time prescribing complete disarmament for a single nation."[1] On the other hand there was a feeling among some Germans, notably socialists and pacifists, that with the removal of Allied control the burden of watching the secret activities of the Reichswehr had been shifted to their own shoulders; because

[1] Stresemann, "Nachlass," 3167/7337/163410 ff. This is a more complete version than the one in Stresemann, *Vermächtnis*, III, 75-76.

89

such activities not only violated international agreements, but they violated German law as well.

This point was clearly stated in a "top secret" memorandum of the Reichswehr Ministry in January 1927. After praising the army for its past efforts at rearmament, carried out by "an alliance of people for the purpose of jointly violating the law . . . a community founded on the holy zeal and spirit of an order," the memorandum expressed admiration for the degree to which in the past "the blurring of the existing fundamental distinction between the lawful tasks of the army and the illegal preparations for mobilization, which had no legal basis whatsoever" had been successful. But there was to be no such "blurring" from now on. "The impending discussions with the Reich Cabinet," the memorandum stated, "on the type and scope of future preparations for mobilization, the planned proposal of the Reich Ministry of Defense for the creation of a council for the defense of the Reich, and the discussions in the Budget Committee of the Reichstag will certainly broach the subject of the international and constitutional legal basis of any preparations for mobilization." Hence it was important to realize, the memorandum continued, that "every soldier or official ordering, directing or executing preparations for mobilization is guilty of violating a Reich law and thus of infringing the military or official duties incumbent on him. A malevolent critic could even reproach him with violating his soldier's oath or oath of office." This fact, the memorandum made clear, was no recent insight. "The competent legal experts," it stated, "had appraised the legal position in this light as early as the winter of 1920-21, when preparations for mobilization were resumed." [2] While the foregoing dealt primarily with illegal activities of persons connected with the armed forces, a separate legal opinion at this

[2] Germany, U. S. Zone of Occupation, Military Tribunals, *Trials of War Criminals*, X, 428-431.

time went further and included civilian members of the government as well. "The members of the Reich government," it said,
"who participate in the preparations for mobilization of a
Wehrmacht exceeding that sanctioned by the Treaty, would
make themselves guilty of an intrastate violation of the Peace
Treaty promulgated as a Reich law," and hence could be
indicted before the State Judicial Court. "In view of the frequent changes of government and considering the uncertain
domestic situation, this possibility should be taken into account." [3]
In other words, the main threat to rearmament from now on
was to be found at home. A socialist government might some
future day prosecute its predecessors for violating the terms of
the Versailles Treaty!

There is no sign that this warning was communicated to the
civilian authorities, though there may be some connection here
with a declaration made by Chancellor Marx in the Reichstag
on February 3. At that time he assured the deputies that any
relations between the Reichswehr and the various patriotic and
paramilitary organizations would from now on be prevented and
that in recruiting new soldiers, candidates loyal to the existing
order would be favored and anti-Republican elements excluded.
"The government," he said, "will pay special attention and
extend special care to the army. (Laughter and shouts on the
left). . . . I want to stress emphatically that in announcing and
carrying out this program I am working in fullest agreement with
the Reichswehrminister and the Chiefs of the Army and Navy.
(Shout from the left: That says everything!)" [4]

But while the Chancellor was thus publicly (and none too
successfully) trying to explain that the Reichswehr's sins were
of the past, Stresemann, in private, spoke quite differently. "I
tell you quite frankly," he confided to a selected audience, "I
should not reproach any German in my soul if he kept the

[3] *Ibid.*, XI, 255.
[4] Germany, Reichstag, *Verhandlungen*, vol. 391, p. 8792.

rifles he has in his house. I do not believe that there is a people in the world that would surrender all of its weapons if an enemy should so demand." And speaking about the Treaty of Versailles in general, he added: "To undermine (aushöhlen) it, to revise it in fact, that is the decisive point."[5]

As far as the disarmament clauses of the Treaty were concerned, this technique of Stresemann's certainly had proved its effectiveness. After the withdrawal of the Allied Control Commission, there remained now only two points on which further negotiations were necessary—the question of eastern fortifications and of German trade in war material. On February 1, the day after the Control Commission had left, Allied and German experts agreed that Germany was to retain some of the new fortifications erected on her eastern and southern borders and that the rest, notably those at Königsberg and Küstrin, were to be destroyed by early summer. As for the trade in war materials, it was decided that a bill should be introduced into the Reichstag defining the articles Germany was forbidden to manufacture, export, or import.[6] In early March the Allies appointed a number of technical experts who were attached to their respective embassies in Berlin in order to see to it that the above agreements were carried out.[7] To do this, however, the experts had to visit Germany's eastern fortifications, so they could verify with their own eyes that the stipulated dismantling had been carried out. Here was a source of renewed conflict. Stresemann told Britain's ambassador in early April that any such visits by military experts would be interpreted as a continuation of military control and hence would cause serious opposition among the German people. The way he himself envisaged the activity of these experts was that they might enquire of the German Foreign Office how far the destruction

[5] Stresemann, "Nachlass," 3167/7338/163659, 163684.
[6] *Schulthess*, vol. 68 (1927), pp. 487-488.
[7] Toynbee, *Survey of International Affairs 1927*, pp. 99-100.

of fortifications had progressed and whether it was nearing completion. Anything more than that, the Foreign Minister added,
would show Allied distrust and with such distrust, no progress
could be made in other fields.[8] But the British were worried
that unless a real inspection of the demolitions in the East could
be made, the French would bring the matter before the League
Council and demand an official investigation, which would only
lead to further complications.[9]

On June 13, the German Foreign Office notified the Allies
that the necessary destructions in the East had been completed;
and as documentary proof the Germans submitted a number of
plans and photographs.[10] But this was not considered sufficient.
The matter came up again between Briand and Stresemann
during the meeting of the League Council in Geneva during
June. The German Foreign Minister insisted that his government "had nothing to hide" and therefore was ready to invite
a neutral representative and perhaps one or two of the Allied
experts to inspect the demolished fortifications. He did not
want to admit all the experts, he said, since that would smack
too strongly of the former Control Commission. And he stressed
that this was the last such Allied action concerned with German
disarmament and that the Allied Conference of Ambassadors,
a "symbol of the war and post-war era," should now be discon-
tinued. Briand could not help expressing his admiration for
his German colleague's strategy. "First," he said, "Herr Strese-
man sends home the military control, and now, bit by bit, he
dissolves the Conference of Ambassadors."[11]

As was to be expected, Stresemann's suggestion won out.
In early July French and Belgian experts under the "guidance"

---

[8] Stresemann, *Vermächtnis*, III, 130-132.
[9] *Ibid.*, pp. 136-137.
[10] Toynbee, *Survey of International Affairs 1927*, p. 100.
[11] Stresemann, *Vermächtnis*, III, 147, 153-154; Stresemann, "Nachlass,"
3170/7344/164413.

of General von Pawelsz, visited the fortresses of Glogau, Küstrin, and Königsberg and reported that the dismantling had been satisfactorily completed.[12] Around this same time, on July 27, a bill specifying the war materials Germany was prohibited from manufacturing, exporting or importing, was passed by the Reichstag,[13] so that, except for a few minor questions, Germany's disarmament obligations at long last had been completed—officially at least. On July 22, 1927, the Conference of Ambassadors sent its final report to the League Council, which henceforth would be the only agency permitted to look into German disarmament violations.[14]

It was very fortunate for Germany that the Allies wound up their supervision when they did; because just at this time, in the early summer of 1927, renewed activities were reported on the part of the so-called 'border guards' (Grenzschutz) along the eastern frontiers. While Stresemann was assuring Briand in Geneva that Germany had nothing to hide, a telegram from Berlin informed him that "certain necessary steps for the protection of the country had been taken in East Prussia," not by setting up local armed units as in 1921, but rather by making "preparations of a personal and material nature for the eventuality of an enemy invasion." The Allies, the report added, had somehow gotten wind of these preparations for mobilization.[15] But if they had, they said nothing. The next reference to the Grenzschutz is contained in a memorandum by Stresemann dealing with a cabinet meeting in September, at which the matter was discussed. "With regard to General Heye's proposals [concerning the Grenzschutz]," Stresemann writes, "I point out that there are no objections, in view of possible Polish attacks,

---

[12] Toynbee, Survey of International Affairs 1927, p. 100.

[13] Germany, U. S. Zone of Occupation, Military Tribunals, Trials of War Criminals, IX, 256 ff.

[14] Schulthess, vol. 68 (1927), p. 489.

[15] Stresemann, "Nachlass," 3148/7343/164375.

to further the *Grenzschutz* as far as is possible under existing agreements."[16] The Foreign Minister certainly had no intention of interfering with the army's activities. Quite the contrary. A few weeks earlier he had thanked Heye for acknowledging his "endeavour to further the Reichswehr," adding that "the one-sided military unpreparedness" of Germany was his "deepest worry."[17]

How far this endeavour of Stresemann's went is shown by another event. In May of 1927, General von Seeckt quietly, but by no means secretly, returned to government service as "adviser on matters of general disarmament and other military-political questions." Seeckt was "hired," if one can use so plebeian a term, not by the Reichswehr, as one might have expected, but by Stresemann and the Foreign Office! The Foreign Minister was not one to bear a grudge towards someone whom, like Seeckt, he respected and in many ways admired. "Stresemann," Seeckt told his wife after his appointment, "was very accommodating, and I shall try, of course, to get along with him and the Foreign Office, in the interest of the cause."[18] In reading Seeckt's account of his new position, one senses a certain embarrassment that he was returning as the protegé of the man he had attacked so mercilessly for many years. He tried to hide this embarrassment by telling his wife that his aid at this point was especially needed, since Germany's foreign position was "so difficult." Financial considerations, an effort to supplement his pension, no doubt played their part in making him accept his new job.[19] But there are also indications that the material and personal disagreements that had separated Seeckt and Strese-

[16] *Ibid.*, 3172/7369/166354.
[17] *Ibid.*, 3170/7346/164800.
[18] Rabenau, *Seeckt*, pp. 626-627. I fail to understand the interpretation of this remark by Seeckt in Bretton, *Stresemann*, p. 145: "This remark would tend to further discount suspicions that Stresemann was a coconspirator in the illegal activities of the army."
[19] Rabenau, *Seeckt*, pp. 626-627.

mann in the past had lost a good deal of their intensity and that
the General's vision, once he was free from the responsibilities of
heading the Reichswehr, expanded beyond the narrow limits
of the purely military. "Armaments races and limitations of
armaments," he wrote in early 1928, "despite their military
appearance, are both political questions. One cannot blame a
soldier for making high demands in regard to fields that are
his responsibility. But to keep these fields within the framework
of a general policy, that is the task of the statesman." [20] And
somewhat later he wrote: "Foreign policy means wrestling with
an adversary, a struggle. Who, in this struggle, can reveal in
advance all his means and methods? Even detours can lead to
the goal." [21] What better description could be given of Stresemann's foreign policy? "We need not always be too careful
about the method [the Foreign Minister had told the German
colony at Geneva in 1926] if only it gets us forward—for in the
end the result decides which is the right one. But we shall only
progress step by step, we shall not always follow a straight path
as might please the more theoretically minded." [22]

But besides these indications that Seeckt at last had come
to understand the circuitous route of Stresemann's foreign policy,
there also were signs that the personal strain between the two
men, which had so adversely affected their official relationship
in the past, was wearing off. As Stresemann's star rose and
Seeckt's fell, their mutual attraction increased. The fact that
both prided themselves on the breadth of their cultural interests
provided a point of contact which became more pronounced as
their social differences lessened. Stresemann's sending a bouquet
of red carnations to Mrs. von Seeckt was termed "very decent"
by the General, and he admonished his wife to pay a call on

[20] Braun, *Von Weimar zu Hitler*, p. 206.
[21] Germany, Heeresarchiv Potsdam, "Papers of General Hans von Seeckt,"
Roll 22 (1930).
[22] Stresemann, *Vermächtnis*, III, p. 28.

the "Stresemänner." There were other amenities between the
two camps: Seeckt giving a complimentary copy of one of his
books to the Foreign Minister, something he did only to a
favored few; Stresemann and Mrs. von Seeckt exchanging their
"ex libris"; Seeckt inviting Stresemann to hear his talk on
"Generalship in Antiquity" and offering to repeat the per-
formance over tea when the Foreign Minister was unable to
attend because of his work. Given time, one feels, these two so
different personalities might have become, if not fast friends,
at least "good acquaintances." [23] As for the professional services
Seeckt rendered in his new capacity, they seem to have con-
sisted primarily in giving occasional opinions on larger questions
of military policy, notably the disarmament problem.[24] He did
not regain the powers he had been forced to relinquish the
previous autumn, nor is there any evidence that he tried to do so
during Stresemann's lifetime.

Contrary to expectations, the year 1927 was not too auspicious
for the army's illegal efforts, despite the fact that the threat of
Allied discovery had once and for all been removed. It was a
year of valiant efforts on the part of the Reichswehr's domestic
critics to throw some light into the darker corners of the army's
past and present activities. As a retrospective survey put it in
1937: "The year 1927 . . . will always have a bad name. . . .
The hand already raised for the forging of arms was stopped
while trying to strike—but only until German men had restored
the situation again and even better than before." [25] One of the
most unsavory secrets of the Reichswehr's early years were the
"Feme" murders committed by members of the "Black Reichs-

[23] For evidence of the Seeckt-Stresemann rapprochement see Rabenau,
Seeckt, p. 638; Stresemann, "Nachlass," 3101/7151/151545; *ibid.*, 3116/
7148/151046; *ibid.*, 3149/7350/165558.
[24] For examples of Seeckt's memoranda see *ibid.*, 3172/7371/166716 ff.;
ibid., 3116/7150/151344 ff.
[25] Germany, U. S. Zone of Occupation, Military Tribunals, *Trials of War
Criminals*, X, 464.

wehr." We have already discussed the first of the "Feme" trials in early 1926. At that time Stresemann had successfully averted public proceedings which might have endangered his foreign policy.[26] During the summer of 1927 the Reichstag appointed a committee to look into the whole "Feme" question and to see to it that the guilty were brought to trial. But as Severing puts it: "Too many groups were interested in preventing an investigation. Thus one poked about in a fog without finding any bodies."[27] There was a feeling among many people, especially on the right, that these gruesome deeds, committed in times of national emergency, should not be dredged up from a murky past. Seeckt, in an informative article on the subject, pleaded on behalf of those who in a period of general confusion had lost "their conception of the value of human life." And he advocated an amnesty for those "Feme" murderers already caught and convicted.[28] In this he was supported by Stresemann, who hoped to avoid all new trials of "Feme" criminals and proposed an amnesty for all other cases except where "actual bestialities were committed."[29]

Aside from the socialists, among the chief domestic critics of the Reichswehr were the pacifists. In their journals, notably Die Menschheit, they revealed in a sometimes overly sensational but basically correct and idealistic manner those activities of the Reichswehr that could not stand the light of day. In doing so, they endangered not only the army, but the foreign policy of Stresemann as well. So it need not surprise us that the agreement between the Foreign Minister and his military colleagues which we already found on such subjects as Grenzschutz and

[26] See above, pp. 49-50.
[27] Severing, Mein Lebensweg, II, 135.
[28] Rabenau, Seeckt, pp. 424-426.
[29] Stresemann, "Nachlass," 3177/7390/170508. Stresemann was particularly interested in having the trial of a Lt. Schulz terminated, "for whose person many important people are interceding." On Schulz's activities see Germany, Reichstag, Verhandlungen, vol. 388, p. 5129.

"Feme," extended to pacifism as well. In August 1927, General Heye asked Stresemann to support a court action the army was bringing against *Die Menschheit* and its editor Friedrich Wilhelm Foerster. Stresemann agreed with alacrity. The journal had just published an article on the relations between the Reichswehr and the patriotic associations, notably the "Stahlhelm," a subject which had caused the Foreign Minister such endless headaches a few months earlier. "I think it an impossible situation," he told Heye, "to permit this journal to continue its activity."[30] In a letter to Foerster's uncle, an octogenarian industrialist, who objected to Stresemann's attacks upon his nephew, Stresemann explained his position in greater detail. "Nothing," he said, "disturbs the policy of understanding between France and Germany more than the continued accusations spread by *Die Menschheit* that Germany is dealing with France dishonestly and on false pretenses, and that the men governing Germany today are only a front behind which stands a Germany armed to the teeth and filled with revenge." And he denounced the accusations in *Die Menschheit* according to which he was supposed to be acquainted with the plan for German rearmament and was contemplating asking the League of Nations for an increase of German armed strength. "Of all these claims," he stated flatly, "not a word is true. Until today I have not the slightest knowledge of this so-called plan."[31] This was written on November 2, 1927, when the Reichswehr's relations with the Red Army, its training of short-term volunteers (*Zeitfreiwillige*), its dealings with the paramilitary patriotic associations and the eastern *Grenzschutz* were far better known to Stresemann than to Friedrich Wilhelm Foerster and his writers on the staff of *Die Menschheit*.

[30] Stresemann, "Nachlass," 3170/7346/164878 ff.; see also Severing, *Mein Lebensweg*, II, 190-191.
[31] Stresemann, *Vermächtnis*, III, 190, 219-221.

The major scandal involving the armed forces came at the end of 1927, and its chief result was the fall of Reichswehrminister Gessler, who had weathered so many storms in the past. The details have no specific bearing on our subject, except for revealing the fact that undercover dealings were not confined to the army but involved the navy as well. In the fall of 1927, a German motion picture company, the "Phoebus Film A.G.," went bankrupt. It was no ordinary company but had been founded and financed with special government funds by a German naval captain, Walter Lohmann, for the purpose of spreading patriotism at home and propaganda abroad. This was not the only enterprise which Lohmann, as administrator of secret naval funds, had embarked upon, but its collapse and the consequent loss to the Reich of vast amounts of money made it the most publicized.[32] The "Phoebus Scandal" naturally was grist to the mill of the army's critics. And to spare the Reichswehr a repetition of the wave of attacks it had faced a year earlier in connection with the Scheidemann revelations, Reichswehrminister Gessler decided to assume the political and parliamentary responsibility for the affair. So on February 14, 1928, he resigned, despite Hindenburg's efforts to make him change his mind. The fact that his relations with the parties of the left, including his own Democratic Party (with which he had severed connections) had steadily deteriorated, and the death of his two sons, helped to influence Gessler's decision.[33] His place was taken by the last Quartermaster General of the Imperial Army, ex-General Groener, who was known for his ability but because of his democratic leanings was persona non grata with some

[32] For an account of Lohmann's activities see Germany, U. S. Zone of Occupation, Military Tribunals, *Trials of War Criminals*, X, 348-355.

[33] Otto Meissner, *Staatssekretär unter Ebert, Hindenburg, Hitler* (Hamburg, 1950), pp. 164-165; Stampfer, *Deutsche Republik*, p. 505. There also were indications of tension between Stresemann and Gessler: Stresemann, "Nachlass," 3115/7143/150297.

of the Reichswehr's older guard.[34] Groener, in all essential respects, proved an able successor to Gessler.

The not inconsiderable difficulties which the army ran into during 1927 were amply balanced by the increasing support it found among the civilian branches of the government. With Allied control out of the way, such support now involved very little risk. It was possible, for instance, in the winter of 1927-28, for the Reichswehr to plan a *Kriegspiel* in close collaboration with the Foreign Office. In December 1927, a discussion was held at the Reichswehr Ministry between members of the army and experts from Stresemann's office on the "political and military situation of the war games scheduled for early next year in which the Foreign Office has been invited to participate." [35] The hypothetical crisis on which the exercise was to be based called for a Polish invasion of East Prussia. The discussion at the time showed that Germany's chances in such an emergency, even under the most favorable international circumstances, were very "dismal." A memorandum on the discussion which was forwarded to Stresemann pointed to this fact as most important "in connection with the question of protective forces [against the East] which at present is under discussion in the Reich cabinet." This eastern *Grenzschutz* continued to occupy a good deal of time in discussions between military and civilian agencies, and the cabinet, in 1929, unanimously accepted new provisions for the eastern border forces, estimated in the vicinity of 30,000 men.[36] Also at this time the agreement which Gessler and Severing had signed on June 30, 1923, for the storage of illegal

[34] The statement in Görlitz, *Generalstab*, p. 376, that "the last Chief of the Great General Staff as President of the Reich thus recalled his last Quartermaster as Reichswehrminister" must not be taken as indication of a conspiracy on Hindenburg's part. The moving spirit behind Groener's appointment was Schleicher. See also Meissner, *Staatssekretär*, pp. 165-166.

[35] Stresemann, "Nachlass," 3165/7414/175357 ff.

[36] Severing, *Mein Lebensweg*, II, 191-192; Braun, *Von Weimar zu Hitler*, p. 267; Görlitz, *Generalstab*, p. 360.

weapons, was extended from Prussia to the rest of Germany, except for the western provinces.[37] Stresemann did not directly participate in any of these negotiations, unless they involved the whole cabinet, in which case it may be assumed that he con-curred in that body's unanimous decisions.

The most important, and as far as our evidence goes, the last of such meetings took place on October 18, 1928. By that time the socialist Hermann Müller had again been made Chancellor, with his party-colleague Severing as Reichsminister of the In-terior, and Stresemann still Minister of Foreign Affairs. The meeting was called by Groener, and its chief purpose was to have General Heye and Admiral Raeder "report openly and fully before all the Ministers as to what breaches [of disarma-ment] there were on the part of the army and the navy." There is a detailed report on the meeting in the transcript of Admiral Raeder's trial before the Nürnberg International Military Tri-bunal in 1946, substantiated in all essential points by Severing's testimony on the same occasion.[38] Severing no longer remem-bered whether Stresemann attended the meeting, but from evidence in the Foreign Minister's unpublished papers it appears quite certain that he was recuperating at the time from one of his frequent illnesses at Wiesbaden in Western Germany. But he must have sent a delegate and thus received a direct report on so vital a conference; and we also know that the information given by Raeder and Heye was later communicated to the members of the cabinet in writing. Raeder in his statements at Nürnberg told how both he and the head of the army had submitted a list of all the individual breaches of the Versailles disarmament provisions to the members of the cabinet, and how

[37] See above p. 9, note 28; also Severing, *Mein Lebensweg*, II, 138, 189.
[38] International Military Tribunal, *Trial of the Major War Criminals* (Nürnberg, 1948), XIII, 621-622; *ibid.*, XIV, 251, 255; *ibid.*, XVIII, 377; see also Severing, *Mein Lebensweg*, II, 137.

"the Müller-Severing-Stresemann government took full responsibility and exonerated the Reich Defense Minister, who, however, continued to be responsible for carrying things through." As for any future measures, they were to be taken only with the knowledge of the Reichswehrminister or the cabinet. According to Severing he and his colleagues assumed these responsibilities because the Reichswehr's violations were "based purely on conceptions of defense"; and Raeder's Defense Counsel added that "even the Prosecution will not desire to assert that men like Stresemann, Müller, and Severing intended to wage wars of aggression." As late as 1946, the peaceful intentions of the Weimar Republic's political leaders were thus cited to minimize the army's breaches of the Treaty of Versailles.

The armed forces at long last had now put their cards on the table. But there are no signs that the revelations they made came as a startling surprise to the cabinet. The meeting, after all, was not called to end the Reichswehr's violations, quite the contrary—it was called to put the heretofore secret and hence haphazard activities of the army and navy on a firmer and more lasting basis, especially as far as finances were concerned. As a later German memorandum described the situation that from now on prevailed in German rearmament: "The work continued now in forceful combination and clever balance of power, and the rearmament was put on a foundation which was more and more expanded by the sharing of the responsibility with the Reich government. The Reich government could not ignore any longer the necessity of this type of work, though the internal political situation did not permit the participation of the Reichsrat and Reichstag." [39]

Thus we come to the end of our discussion. German secret

[39] Germany, U. S. Zone of Occupation, Military Tribunals, *Trials of War Criminals*, X, 464.

rearmament continued, of course, throughout the few remaining years of the Weimar Republic until it gained really full force under the Nazis. But as it became generally accepted (or better, ignored) abroad and no longer posed a threat to Stresemann's foreign policy, the Foreign Minister could devote his attention to more urgent problems. He had rung down the curtain on German "disarmament" in a speech before the Reichstag on June 23, 1927. The German police, he claimed at that time, had been reorganized according to Allied wishes; patriotic associations that engaged in military practices had been dissolved; the required demolition of eastern fortifications had taken place; in short, Stresemann concluded, " our own disarmament to the point of bareness and the guarantees which are contained in the treaties of Locarno are the most extreme one can offer one's neighbors in the way of security." [40] Yet Stresemann's speech not only asserted German disarmament, it also pointed to the next major task he had set himself—the achievement of universal disarmament, or, as he conceived it, equality of armament for Germany. Because important as Germany's violations of the disarmament clauses had been and continued to be, they merely laid the groundwork for the ultimate expansion from Reichswehr to Wehrmacht and did not in themselves create an army comparable to those of the other major powers. As a memorandum of the British General Staff summed up the situation in 1932: " Such military preparations as have been made by the German nation in contravention of the treaty are mainly defensive in character. It will not be possible, at all events, for Germany to contemplate an aggressive war upon France until the treaty restrictions have been removed (including those relating to the Rhineland), or, alternatively, until Germany is in a position to denounce them with impunity. In existing circumstances, the

[40] Germany, Reichstag, *Verhandlungen*, vol. 393, pp. 11001 ff.

General Staff cannot believe that Germany is at present in a position to defend herself successfully against France and Belgium, even if Poland and Czechoslovakia did not intervene." In other words, the British General Staff agreed that Germany's military preparations during the Weimar period had been primarily defensive, and as such by no means sufficient to protect Germany against another great power. "It is the realization of her present military weakness," the memorandum concluded, "which is at the root of the German demand for equality of treatment in the sphere of armaments." [41]

This realization certainly had been in Stresemann's mind for some time. After liberating his country from the restrictions of Allied military control, the Foreign Minister had worked successfully for the evacuation of Allied occupation forces from the Rhineland ahead of schedule. This victory, which he won in drawn-out and exhausting wranglings with Briand at the Hague Conference in August 1929, came on the eve of his death. It too was a step further along the road back to absolute German sovereignty in the military field; although the demilitarization of the Rhineland continued until, in the words of the British General Staff, Germany could "denounce it with impunity," which Hitler did in 1936. The more immediate task in 1929 was to make progress with general disarmament. "From the tenor and contents of his last address before the League, it was clear that Stresemann, had he been permitted to live, would have concentrated on the theme of universal disarmament, permitting the disarmament clauses of the peace treaty to remain dead letters." [42] But it is also clear, as was pointed out above, that the term disarmament in Stresemann's mind was synony-

[41] Great Britain, Foreign Office, *Documents on British Foreign Policy 1919-1939*, edited by E. L. Woodward and Rohan Butler, Second Series, vol. III, 1931-32 (London, 1948), p. 605.
[42] Bretton, *Stresemann*, p. 147; Stresemann, *Vermächtnis*, III, 574-575.

mous with equality of armament for Germany. In other words, the problem was to get the rest of the powers to disarm down to Germany's level, or else get their permission to have Germany rearm up to their level. Which of these alternatives was closer to Stresemann's heart, the reader will have to decide on the basis of the evidence presented in this study.[43]

---

[43] Bretton, *Stresemann*, p. 145, concludes that Stresemann " knew of the secret rearmament conducted by the army and was well aware of the armament capacity of German industry. There was hope, however, if his campaign for universal disarmament succeeded, that the German public could be persuaded to embrace international conciliation, and that the nationalists would lose ground in Germany." This writer does not share this optimistic view. Nor does he agree with Bretton's statement, *ibid.*, p. 146: " Whether Stresemann was directly involved in the violations and breaches of the peace treaty or not, and recently uncovered evidence would indicate that he was not . . . ," which three pages later (*ibid.*, p. 149) evolves into the assertion: " Stresemann . . . was not directly involved in the actual rearmament of Germany by clandestine means."

VI | Conclusion

THE PURPOSE of this study has been first of all to illustrate
in the person of Gustav Stresemann, the degree to which Germany's secret rearmament during the Weimar Republic was
carried on in collaboration between military and civilian agencies.
The key position which Stresemann occupied as Foreign
Minister, his uninterrupted service during six crucial years, and
the fact that in his collected papers we have a better key to
his thoughts and actions than is available for any other figure,
these facts combined made Stresemann the most promising
subject for our examination. Occasional glimpses at other leading personalities of the Weimar period, however, have shown
sufficiently that Stresemann's attitude toward secret rearmament,
which ranged from passive acceptance to active assistance, was
not unique. Though in the case of men like Wirth and Cuno,
such acquiescence and aid was given in periods of acute national
crisis; and in the case of Severing, it was granted with some
misgivings and to meet the real or imaginary threats of communist
uprising at home and Polish invasion from abroad. All these
motives we have also noted on Stresemann's part, but there
were others besides.

This brings up a second and equally important purpose, which
is to make a contribution to our understanding of one of
Germany's great statesmen. Stresemann's biographers, whether
writing in 1928 or 1952, have been so impressed by their
subject's apparent metamorphosis from ardent nationalist to
internationalist, that they have accepted this change as the pre-

determined theme for their work . The fact that several of them
had known and liked the man, and the sympathy which even
the most critical historian must feel for the devotion and courage
with which Stresemann served his country, sacrificing wealth,
health, and finally his life to that cause, merely aided the acceptance of this theme. But in their effort to bring consistency into
the story of Stresemann's eventful and contradictory career, his
biographers, blinded by admiration or bound by their thesis, have
omitted some important sides of his many-faceted personality
and policy. With one of them, this study is concerned.

Aside from Stresemann, it also deals with German disarmament and/or rearmament. If these terms have been used inter-
changeably, it is due to the fact that the line between Germany's
failures to disarm and her efforts to rearm is often difficult to
draw. We cannot here go into the justification for these German
military activities. Their defenders have cited the Allied failure
of complementing German disarmament with reduction of their
own forces, and the resulting danger which a "military vacuum"
in the heart of Europe presented to world peace by inviting
outside aggression or domestic uprising. These external and
internal dangers may have been exaggerated, but to many
Germans who remembered the early postwar years the threat of
a Polish invasion or a communist uprising nevertheless appeared
quite real. On the other hand, the fact remains that Germany
in her clandestine operations violated the military clauses of
the Versailles Treaty and several subsequent minor agreements
and promises. Both German and foreign observers agree that
Germany's military breaches of the Treaty were defensive in
character. Yet such judgments are based primarily on quantita-
tive considerations. Given the necessary funds and an all-out
national effort, Seeckt's and Heye's defensive Reichswehr, as
events since 1933 have shown, could in surprisingly short order
be transformed into Hitler's aggressive Wehrmacht. Needless
to say, there is no evidence that Stresemann envisaged such a
transformation.

What exactly did he envisage? This brings us to the most important part of our effort at deriving some conclusions from our findings. From the evidence that has been presented it should be abundantly clear that Stresemann supported, at times actively and always in his heart, any move on the army's part that tended to remedy Germany's military impotence. He did so partly because of all the army had meant to Germany in the past—in other words, Stresemann was a nationalist and there is ample evidence that he remained one to the end of his life; although his nationalism became more moderate and tolerant as he grew in stature. But more decisive than such personal admiration for things military in shaping Stresemann's attitude were reasons of state. Among all the various elements which determine a country's international rank, from size and geographic location to natural resources and industrial potential, the possession of a powerful army has always proved the most immediately effective. As Stresemann once put it: "The main asset [of a strong foreign policy] is material power—army and navy."[1] One would therefore expect that a nation, defeated in war but still feeling entitled to a place among the great powers, would try to regain not only its former political and economic strength, but that it would also aim to save as much as possible of its military machinery and soon again try to regain its military strength; not necessarily to use such strength for a forcible reversal of the verdict of war, but perhaps, by a little judicious rattling of sabres, to gain a more favorable hearing in the councils of the great for the "peaceful" revision of that verdict. In other words, in trying to free the Reichswehr from Allied supervision and in not obstructing its relations with the Red Army, Stresemann was simply doing what any patriotic statesman would have done in any other country. It was only due to the desire of his biographers and many of his contempo-

[1] Stresemann, "Nachlass," 3144/7323/160742.

raries (especially outside Germany) to find some incarnation, some symbol for their belief that a new era had dawned in the relationship between great powers, that the prevalent overly idealized picture of Stresemann has been drawn and that any effort to see the warts on his nose has been branded as defamation. Actually a disservice was thus rendered the man. Because as evidence appeared which contradicted this shining image in some respects, there now were writers who claimed that it was false in all respects.

But to say simply that Stresemann favored a strong army as a potent factor in an effective foreign policy, while basically correct, still overlooks most of the intricacies of the situation he had to face. The root of Germany's greatness, in Stresemann's opinion, lay in her inherent economic strength. His confidence in the irresistibility of German economic expansion, which can be traced back to his early years as Reichstag deputy, never seems to have left him. But such expansion necessitated economic recovery at home and the reintegration of Germany into the world market. And hand in hand with such economic revival a lessening of tension had to take place in the political field. Stresemann's achievements in these respects were truly remarkable. Not only was he able to effect a political rapprochement with the West, but he also managed to continue the friendly relations with the Soviet Union, initiated by his predecessors. The Locarno Treaties of 1925 and the Treaty of Berlin of 1926 are testimony to his amazing dexterity in maneuvering between the East and West.[2] In the economic field he was equally successful in lessening the burden of reparations and helping to attract the foreign capital necessary for Germany's renaissance.[3]

[2] Professor Otto Hoetzsch, usually quite critical of Stresemann's policy, hailed the conclusion of the Russo-German Treaty of Berlin as comparable to Bismarck's famous Re-insurance Treaty: Stresemann, " Nachlass," 3145/7326/161346.

[3] As early as 1925 Stresemann predicted, in private, that Germany in all

It was these achievements that established his fame everywhere
as a man of moderation and circumspection; everywhere, that
is, except among the rightist and monarchist opposition in his
own country.

To the German Nationalists behind Hugenberg, to the
growing number of Hitler's followers, and even to many members of his own People's Party, Stresemann's policy of fulfillment (or of "liberation," as he preferred to call it) appeared
unworthy of a great power, and instead of liberating Germany
from foreign enslavement it merely tended, in the opinion of
these groups, to perpetuate her present inferiority. It was these
circles from whom the officer corps as well as most of the rank
and file of the German Reichswehr were recruited, and who
made up the vast paramilitary and patriotic associations in which
postwar Germany abounded. And their activities and vociferous
opposition in turn endangered Stresemann's efforts in the political
and economic field. The ideal procedure in leading Germany
back to a position of greatness would have been to do first things
first—to complete the political *détente* and economic recovery,
and then try to regain military strength. But the impatience
of many of his countrymen forced Stresemann to pursue two
conflicting courses simultaneously. On the one hand he tried,
successfully, to win back international confidence in the peaceful
intentions of his policy, while on the other he had to give as
much support as he dared to the Reichswehr's efforts at secretly
breaking the military restrictions of Versailles. If this policy was
two-faced, that was not entirely Stresemann's fault. Without
such support, and without such occasional triumphs as the termination of Allied military control or the evacuation of the Rhine-

probability would not live up to her reparations obligations under the Dawes
Plan. At the same time he stressed the desirability of becoming and remaining
a " debtor nation," so as to assure continued interest abroad in Germany's
economic well-being. Needless to say, he did not broadcast these views:
ibid., 3144/7323/160745 ff.

land, his efforts at the political and economic rehabilitation of Germany would have foundered on the opposition of the right. To this extent, but to this extent only, was Stresemann's favorable attitude to German rearmament forced upon him by circumstances. To go further, however, and say that he was fundamentally opposed to such rearmament would be wrong. Had the Reichswehr's aims and activities run counter to his convictions, he could (and in view of his forthright character he probably would) have adopted a quite different course. He might have aligned himself still more closely with those political groups of the center and left who supported his foreign policy and were critical of the Reichswehr's activities and he might have tried to use the prestige his foreign policy had gained him to force the cessation of the army's undercover activities. If this had proved unsuccessful, and it probably would have, he could have done what other men of principle have done under similar circumstances—he could have resigned. But the policy Stresemann pursued, while perhaps not in all respects of his choice, did not run counter to his convictions. Its very difficulty provided a challenge to the consummate skill with which he handled foreign affairs. In trying the seemingly impossible, pursuing appeasement abroad while supporting rearmament at home, he always had to be aware that one might defeat the other. Although as we have seen, the eagerness of the British and of a man like Briand to believe in the moderation and good will of Stresemann made the latter's tasks a good deal easier. Still he could never relax his watchfulness and enjoy the relief of explaining to his countrymen the intricacies of his policy, for fear that its long-range aims would thus leak out and disillusion his foreign admirers. "Giving way in silence, in order to husband the future, suppressing strong words, which relieve the anger of a democracy, but warn the enemy: for such methods calm and coolheaded men with self-control are needed: dangerous men." This was how Jacques Bainville, that astute observer of the

German scene, had described Stresemann as far back as 1921.[4]
"The Foreign Minister who remains silent on certain matters,"
Stresemann said in 1926, "is more important than the one who
talks about everything."[5]

What were Stresemann's ultimate aims? It is here that we are
still on somewhat uncertain ground, and probably will remain
so until we gain access to the files of the German Foreign Office
for the Weimar period. We have already cited the famous
letter of September 7, 1925, to the former German Crown
Prince which, even with all the new material we now have, is
still one of the clearest expositions of his aims Stresemann ever
wrote; though even here he dared not speak as freely as he
would have liked to, and as an added precaution he did not
sign his name to the letter.[6] There is nothing in it that one
could not find elsewhere in his unpublished writings, but never
in this frank and condensed form.[7] The immediate and long-
range aims of German foreign policy, according to Stresemann,
were as follows: to free Germany from Allied occupation; "the
solution of the reparations question in a sense tolerable to
Germany"; "the protection of Germans abroad, those 10-12
million *Stammesgenossen* living under a foreign yoke"; "the
readjustment of our Eastern frontiers—the recovery of Danzig,
the Polish corridor and a correction of the frontier of Upper
Silesia"; "in the background stands the union with German
Austria, although I am clear that this not merely brings no
advantage to Germany, but seriously complicates the problem of
the German Reich"; "moreover, all the questions that lie so
close to German hearts, as for instance war guilt, general disarma-

[4] Quoted in Scheele, *The Weimar Republic*, p. 235.

[5] Stresemann, "Nachlass," 3167/7336/163095.

[6] Stresemann, "Nachlass," 3168/7318/159871 ff.

[7] For an equally remarkable, though much more voluminous statement of
Stresemann's aims, see his speech of Dec. 14, 1925, to the "Arbeitsgemeinschaft Deutscher Landsmannschaften," *ibid.*, 3144/7323/160742 ff.

ment, Danzig, the Saar, etc., are matters for the League of
Nations, and a skillful speaker at a plenary session of the League
may make them very disagreeable for the Entente." And at
the end of his letter Stresemann said that German foreign policy
must "finassieren" and "avoid big decisions," in other words:
it had to achieve by finesse what it could not gain by force.
There was a joke that went the rounds about the time this
letter was written which Stresemann enjoyed sufficiently to file
with his papers: Stresemann: "We have no more territorial
claims." Pacifist: "I knew it!" Stresemann: "The borders of
1914 are perfectly adequate for us."[8] Except for Alsace-
Lorraine, which was not included in the claims enumerated in
the letter to the Crown Prince, the joke pretty much covers the
aims of that document; and the loss of the two provinces was
amply balanced by the demand for an Austrian Anschluss. Nor
did Stresemann exclude the possibility of a return of Alsace-
Lorraine. His statement on this subject to the Crown Prince
is quite ambiguous: The Locarno Pact, it says, "contains the
renunciation of a warlike controversy with France over the
return of Alsace-Lorraine, a German renunciation which has
only theoretical significance, however, since there is no possibility of a war against France." Elsewhere Stresemann had
hinted that such renunciation was not "for all eternity" but
for one generation at best.[9] The Locarno agreements, he had
told the German cabinet, were not concluded "to stabilize the
status quo," but "to assure peace"; and they did not include
any "relinquishment of former German territory."[10]

We mention these things here to remind ourselves what the
aims were which a Germany, economically powerful and mili-
tarily at least as strong as the other powers, would have pursued.

[8] *Ibid.*, 3100/7137/149372.
[9] *Ibid.*, 3143/7315/159330; *ibid.*, 3113/7131/148414; *ibid.*, 3144/7323/
160763.
[10] *Ibid.*, 3169/7319/160160.

Whether in the fulfillment of Stresemann's long-range program the actual use of force was envisaged, is impossible to say, and the historian must guard here against the dangers of hindsight. There is no evidence even that Stresemann felt his objectives could all be attained in his own lifetime. And there is ample evidence that, at least while Germany was still weak, he favored peaceful arbitration over a forcible showdown as a means of achieving his ends. This does not exclude, however, an awareness of the advantages which a strong army afforded a determined negotiator. Though again there is no evidence that Stresemann foresaw the lengths to which these advantages could be pressed by a man like Hitler.

The picture of Stresemann that emerges from all we have said, then, is that of a great German statesman, the greater perhaps for the two-faced policy which devotion to his country and the belief in its future made him pursue, and which at the same time was so at variance with his upright character as an individual.[11] Yet he was not the "good European," the "honest dreamer of peace and apostle of reconciliation," as he appeared to many of his contemporaries and most of his biographers. We might call him a "good European" if we thought of Europe as ending on the Vistula. Or we might say he was as good a European as Bismarck had been, the one among his predecessors to whom he has often been compared, whose concept of Realpolitik he admired, and with whom he shared the realization that politics is the art of the possible. But when all is said and done, truly good Europeans are extremely rare, and one should least expect to find them among politicians of a defeated country in an age where nationalism is still a potent force.

[11] As Carr, *German-Soviet Relations*, pp. 189-190, points out: "It is customary for foreign ministers to deny all knowledge of the secret operations of other departments—or even of their own; and it would be unfair to attribute these official deceptions to any personal idiosyncrasy in Stresemann's character. Few statesmen fail in an emergency to recognize a duty to lie for their country."

In the final analysis, of course, a monograph of this kind cannot really arrive at definite conclusions about the aims and achievements of a man as complex as Stresemann. It can merely hope to aid future biographers whose task will be to see his whole foreign policy against its domestic background and to determine how much final weight should be assigned to his relations with Germany's armed forces and their illegal activities. It is hoped that in such efforts to discover the real Stresemann behind the legend that has grown up around him, this little book will prove of some value.

Bibliographical note

LORD D'ABERNON once described his friend Stresemann as "more remarkable for the distrust he arouses than for the admiration and confidence he inspires." While this may have been true in Stresemann's lifetime, there is little if any trace of such distrust in the biographies written about him. Their number, by now, is quite impressive. The first to appear was Rochus Freiherr von Rheinbaben, *Stresemann: Der Mensch und der Staatsmann* (Dresden, 1928), written with Stresemann's help. It was followed in quick succession by: Rudolf Olden, *Stresemann* (Berlin, 1929); Heinrich Bauer, *Stresemann, ein deutscher Staatsmann* (Berlin, 1930), corrected by Stresemann's secretary Henry Bernhard; and Antonina Vallentin, *Stresemann, das Werden einer Staatsidee* (Leipzig, 1930), republished with an epilogue by Henry Bernhard (Munich and Leipzig, 1947). The flood was temporarily halted by the Nazi interlude (except for Edgar Stern-Rubarth, *Three Men Tried . . . Austen Chamberlain, Stresemann, Briand* [London, 1939]), only to recommence after the Second World War, with Walter Görlitz, *Gustav Stresemann* (Heidelberg, 1947), the most informative of the biographies; Hubertus Prinz zu Löwenstein, *Stresemann. Das deutsche Schicksal im Spiegel seines Lebens* (Frankfurt a. M., 1952); and the forthcoming book by Annelise Thimme, "Gustav Stresemann, Im Kampf um den Weimarer Staat." All these authors with the notable exception of Miss Thimme (whose well-balanced book, however, does not claim to be definitive) openly admit their admiration for their subject and hence shed a good deal more warmth than light.[1] The authoritative scholarly biography of Stresemann has yet to be written.

[1] Gerhard Zwoch, *Gustav Stresemann. Ein europäischer Staatsmann,* had been announced but not published when this study went to press.

At the same time, there is an abundance of material available, both published and unpublished, for the writing of such a book. Stresemann's published writings have been listed in the admirable bibliography of Gerhard Zwoch, *Gustav-Stresemann-Bibliographie* (Düsseldorf, 1953) which is less complete, however, on secondary works dealing with Stresemann. The major published source on Stresemann's official career between 1923 and 1929 is the three volumes of his papers, Gustav Stresemann, *Vermächtnis. Der Nachlass in drei Bänden*, ed. by Henry Bernhard (Berlin, 1932-33); the English edition, *Gustav Stresemann, His Diaries, Letters, and Papers*, edited and translated by Eric Sutton, 3 vols. (London, 1935-40), has been slightly condensed. As might be expected from the early date at which they appeared and from the close relations between Stresemann and Bernhard, the material in these massive tomes has been carefully screened so as not to interfere with the favorable picture of Stresemann already prevalent in his biographies. How far this process of selection was carried did not become plain until after the Second World War, when the papers of the Foreign Minister came into Allied hands as part of the vast collection of German Foreign Office materials. In 1953 a microfilm of these papers: Germany, Auswärtiges Amt, Politisches Archiv, "Nachlass des Reichsministers Dr. Gustav Stresemann," was made available by the Department of State at the National Archives, Washington, D. C. We cannot here discuss in detail the immense value of this source, not only for a better understanding of Stresemann, but also for the history of Germany in the first three decades of this century. (See Hans W. Gatzke, "The Stresemann Papers," *Journal of Modern History*, XXVI, No. 1 [March 1954].) About half of the papers deal with the period before 1923, on which the *Vermächtnis* says very little, and the rest contains much that has been omitted in the *Vermächtnis*. Until further unpublished sources become available, the "Nachlass" will remain the most important source for any study of Stresemann.

The subject of German illegal rearmament during the Weimar Republic likewise has not as yet been thoroughly treated. J. H. Morgan, *Assize of Arms* (London, 1945), originally planned as a two-volume work, never went beyond the first, largely introductory volume, and plans for its promising sequel have been abandoned. Herbert Rosinski, *The German Army* (Washington, 1944); Telford Taylor, *Sword and Swastika* (New York, 1952); Walter Görlitz, *Der Deutsche Generalstab* (Frankfurt a. M., 1950); and John Wheeler-Bennett, *The Nemesis of Power* (London, 1953), each devote one or more chapters to the Weimar period, but none covers the whole subject. Also useful, as a general introduction, are the relevant chapters (V–VIII) in Godfrey Scheele, *The Weimar Republic* (London, 1946). Some valuable material presented as evidence at the Nürnberg war crimes trials on pre-Hitler rearmament can be found in: International Military Tribunal, *Trial of the Major War Criminals*, vols. XIII, XIV, XVIII (Nürnberg, 1948), and in: Germany, U. S. Zone of Occupation, *Trials of War Criminals before the Nürnberg Military Tribunals*, vols. IX and X (Government Printing Office, Washington, D. C., 1950-51). On the activities of the Inter-Allied Military Control Commission both General Morgan's *Assize of Arms*, and General C. N. E. Nollet, *Une Expérience de désarmement* (Paris, 1932) give accounts based on their own experiences as members of that Commission. As far as Allied-German negotiations over disarmament and Allied military control are concerned, the pertinent volumes of the *Survey of International Affairs*, ed. by Arnold J. Toynbee or C. A. Macartney, under the auspices of the Royal Institute of International Affairs, and of *Schulthess' Europäischer Geschichtskalender*, ed. by Ulrich Thürauf, present valuable summaries and the most important documents. The secret relations between the Reichswehr and Russia are treated in Edward Hallet Carr, *German-Soviet Relations between the Two World Wars 1919-1939* (Baltimore, 1951), and in the basic article by Helm Speidel, "Reichswehr und Rote Armee," *Vierteljahrshefte für Zeitgeschichte*, I, No. 1 (January 1953). Other valuable contributions to the subject include: George W. F. Hallgarten, "General Hans von Seeckt and Russia, 1920-1922," *Journal of Modern History*, XXI, No. 1 (March 1949); Julius Epstein, "Der Seeckt Plan," *Der Monat*, I, No. 2 (November 1948); and Gustav Hilger and Alfred G. Meyer, *The Incompatible Allies—A Memoir-History of German-Soviet Relations 1918-1941* (New York, 1953).

All the works cited thus far have proved very useful in the prep-

aration of the present study, though its specific subject, Stresemann's relations to German rearmament, is not adequately covered
in any of them. A brief chapter on "Disarmament and Revision"
in Henry L. Bretton, *Stresemann and the Revision of Versailles*
(Stanford, 1953) does not permit any thorough analysis of this
important side of the Foreign Minister's career. The major source
proved to be Stresemann's unpublished "Nachlass," and its considerably shorter published version, the *Vermächtnis* (if checked
against the original papers); though the references Stresemann made
to rearmament in writing are far from abundant. There was the
constant fear on the part of everyone involved, that news of the
Reichswehr's secret operations might leak out. And as Severing
once put it: "If one writes it down, it is as good as betrayed." For
the same reason the unpublished papers of Generals von Seeckt and
Groener (on microfilm at Widener Library, Harvard University,
Cambridge, Massachusetts) and the memoirs of Field Marshal von
Blomberg (on deposit at the Federal Records Center, Alexandria,
Virginia) contain very little on rearmament. On Stresemann's
relations with Seeckt, Friedrich von Rabenau, *Seeckt: Aus seinem
Leben 1918-1936* (Leipzig, 1940) is the most useful, despite obvious
flaws due to the fact that it was written during the Nazi period
and by a friend of Seeckt's. It should be supplemented by Reginald
H. Phelps, "Aus den Seeckt-Dokumenten II," *Deutsche Rundschau*,
LXXVIII, No. 10 (October 1952), and by the less valuable article
by Henry Bernhard, "Seeckt und Stresemann," *Deutsche Rundschau*, LXXIX, No. 5 (May 1953). For Stresemann's early contacts
with the Reichswehr, the dissertation by Erich Heinz Schlottner,
*Stresemann, der Kapp Putsch und die Ereignisse in Mitteldeutsch-
land und in Bayern im Herbst 1923* (Frankfurt a. M., 1948), despite
the fact that the author did not have access to Stresemann's "Nachlass," is very good. The memoirs of most German statesmen of the
Weimar Republic rarely touch on the question of German rearmament, and if so, only in the most general terms. An exception is
Carl Severing, *Mein Lebensweg*, 2 vols. (Cologne, 1950), which
shows that knowledge of and aid to the Reichswehr's clandestine
activities extended even to socialist circles. Other works worth
mentioning, in the order of their usefulness to this study, are:

Friedrich Stampfer, *Die ersten vierzehn Jahre der Deutschen Republik* (2d ed., Offenbach, 1947); Otto Braun, *Von Weimar zu Hitler* (New York, 1940); and Otto Meissner, *Staatssekretär unter Ebert, Hindenburg, Hitler* (Hamburg, 1950). Among non-German statesmen, the most important account relevant to our subject is the memoirs of Britain's ambassador Viscount D'Abernon, *The Diary of an Ambassador*, 3 vols. (New York, 1929-31), which prove him to be the trusting friend of Stresemann's on the subject of German disarmament that he was on most other subjects.

Finally there remain several sources of potential significance which for one reason or another could not be consulted. The archives of Stresemann's German People's Party, at present in the Russian Zone of Germany; the minutes of the Reichstag's Foreign Affairs Committee, available in the Bavarian Staatskanzlei; and most important, the documents of the German Foreign Office for the Weimar period, which are in the hands of the German Foreign Ministry Documents project, sponsored by the U. S., British, and French governments. It would be a major service to historical scholarship if this last source could soon be opened for research to qualified scholars.

Index

Index

Adenauer, K., 30
Air force, see Aviation
Allied Commission, see Inter-Allied Military Control Commission
Allied Conference of Ambassadors, 19, 21, 23, 28, 31, 54, 57, 61, 70 f., 93, 94
Allied Control Commission, see Inter-Allied Military Control Commission
Allied military experts and German rearmament, 46, 56 f., 66, 71
Allies: disagreements over German disarmament, 31, 35, 47; and Russo-German military relations, 72, 75, 86
Alsace-Lorraine, 114
Anschluss, 51, 113, 114. See also, Austria
Arbeitsgemeinschaft deutscher Landsmannschaften, 113 n.
Arbeitsgemeinschaften, 16 n.
Arbeitskommandos, 16 n.
Armament industry, 9, 29, 33
Arms, see War material

Army, see Reichswehr, Wehrmacht, "Black Reichswehr"
Associations, see Patriotic organizations
Austria, 51 f., 53, 113
Aviation: civilian, 32, 45 n.; military, 9 n., 54, 69, 80, 81

Bainville, J., 112
Baltimore Sun, 75
Bauer, H., Stresemann, ein deutscher Staatsmann, 117
Bauer, Col. M., 5
Bavaria, 14, 17
Belgium, 105
Berlin, Treaty of, 110
Berliner Tageblatt, 30, 85
Berndorf, H. R., General zwischen Ost und West, 59 n.
Bernhard, H., 4, 50, 59 n., 82, 117, 118; "Seeckt und Stresemann," 11 n., 120
Bethmann Hollweg, Th. von, 11
Bieligk, K. F., Stresemann. The German Liberals' Foreign Policy, 5 n.

125